Construction of Elliptic Curves with Complex Multiplication

Özkan Canbay

Construction of Elliptic Curves with Complex Multiplication

Applied to Primality Testing

Formal Sciences Series

Impressum / Imprint

Bibliografische Information der Deutschen Nationalbibliothek: Die Deutsche Nationalbibliothek verzeichnet diese Publikation in der Deutschen Nationalbibliografie; detaillierte bibliografische Daten sind im Internet über http://dnb.d-nb.de abrufbar.

Alle in diesem Buch genannten Marken und Produktnamen unterliegen warenzeichen-, marken- oder patentrechtlichem Schutz bzw. sind Warenzeichen oder eingetragene Warenzeichen der jeweiligen Inhaber. Die Wiedergabe von Marken, Produktnamen, Gebrauchsnamen, Handelsnamen, Warenbezeichnungen u.s.w. in diesem Werk berechtigt auch ohne besondere Kennzeichnung nicht zu der Annahme, dass solche Namen im Sinne der Warenzeichen- und Markenschutzgesetzgebung als frei zu betrachten wären und daher von jedermann benutzt werden dürften.

Bibliographic information published by the Deutsche Nationalbibliothek: The Deutsche Nationalbibliothek lists this publication in the Deutsche Nationalbibliografie; detailed bibliographic data are available in the Internet at http://dnb.d-nb.de.

Any brand names and product names mentioned in this book are subject to trademark, brand or patent protection and are trademarks or registered trademarks of their respective holders. The use of brand names, product names, common names, trade names, product descriptions etc. even without a particular marking in this works is in no way to be construed to mean that such names may be regarded as unrestricted in respect of trademark and brand protection legislation and could thus be used by anyone.

Coverbild / Cover image: www.ingimage.com

Verlag / Publisher:
AV Akademikerverlag GmbH & Co. KG
Heinrich-Böcking-Str. 6-8, 66121 Saarbrücken, Deutschland / Germany
Email: info@akademikerverlag.de

Herstellung: siehe letzte Seite /
Printed at: see last page
ISBN: 978-3-639-44975-4

Abstract

An abstract model of an elliptic curve is designed as a Java-based application. In this abstract model we implement two distinct elliptic curve types: the Weierstraß curve and the twisted Edwards curve. This model will be used in the algorithm for elliptic curve construction with complex multiplication, in short the CM-method. We implement the elliptic curve primality proving algorithm (ECPP) developed by Atkin/Morain as an application of the CM-method. Instead of using pseudocode, the algorithms are represented explicitly as source code simultaneously with the underlying theory. Finally, we analyze a probable acceleration of the Atkin-Morain's ECPP algorithm by replacing the Weierstraß curve by the twisted Edwards curve.

Acknowledgements

I would like to thank my supervisors Prof. Dr. Steffen Reith and Dr. Rasa Steuding for their support during the work on this thesis. Prof. Dr. Reith offered me valuable guidance and advice, whenever I needed it. Dr. Rasa Steuding introduced me to the theory of elliptic curves, enabling me to successfully read and utilize scientific reviews on that topic. Her thought-provoking questions provided impulses that helped me to improve the results of this thesis.

I also wish to acknowledge the support of my friend and colleaque, Dr.Markus Grabowski. He became tremendously interested in the theory of elliptic curves and was always willing to discuss it in detail. That helped me to consider the topic from other perspectives.

Finally, I want to thank my wife Marion and our children Amelie and Kilian for understanding that after work I often had to withdraw to my office to work on this master thesis.

Contents

Contents

Chapter 1.

Introduction

One central subject of this thesis is to demonstrate the elegance and power of object oriented programming by applying it to a very abstract subject at the center of mathematics. The subject is elliptic curves. Elliptic curves appear in many diverse areas of mathematics, with applications ranging from complex analysis, number theory, algebra to geometry. Elliptic curves, which originated from elliptic functions founded by Euler, Abel, Jacobi, Weierstraß and many others, is still an active field of research. The main interest in elliptic curves is focused on their group structures.

For example, elliptic curves played a central role in the proof of Fermat's last theorem by Andrew Wiles et al. Another example and still an open problem is the Birch/Swinnerton-Dyer conjecture concerning certain properties of the group structure of elliptic curves. It is an application of the local-global principle, i.e. the possibility to make a statement about the group structure of an elliptic curves over a *large* field derived from the simpler properties of the curve restricted to a finite field. The conjecture is one of the millenium problems of the Clay Mathematics Institute.

Recently the research of elliptic curves experienced an additional motivation through applications of elliptic curves in cryptography. Elliptic curve cryptography (ECC) is today a common approach. The main advantage of ECC is, it uses smaller key size while providing the same level of security compared to classical crypto-systems.

The research on cryptography with respect to elliptic curves created many algorithms based on fundamental theorems of elliptic curve theory. However, the elegance of the fundamental theorems is not fully reflected in many of the implementations. Although the mathematical concepts deal with mathematical objects and structures, the implementations are mostly realized procedurally.

In this thesis, we try to preserve the mathematical objects and structures in the implementations. We believe, this reflection can be achieved by using the object oriented approach.

The thesis is divided into three topics. In the first topic, we will introduce elliptic curves and their arithmetic properties. Beginning with the reference model for the elliptic curve, denoted as Weierstraß curve, we introduce the group structure and main arithmetic properties. Next, we discuss in detail Hasse's theorem, which gives a boundary for the number of points of an elliptic curve over a finite field. At the end of the first topic, we introduce a further model of an elliptic curve, denoted as the twisted Edwards curve. Due to their symmetrical appearence, twisted Edwards curves are believed to have some arithmetical advantages compared to Weierstraß

Chapter 1. Introduction

curves leading to faster algorithms. After analyzing the similarities and differences of these two types of elliptic curves, we will develop an object-oriented model for a general elliptic curve structure by using the *top-down* strategy. We will add the Weierstraß curve and twisted Edwards curve to this model. Since every additional curve only has to implement/extend certain interface/abstract class, it will be convenient to extend the model to further curve types. The final tool will be called the *elliptic curve arithmetic system* and will be taken as a basis for the other two topics.

In the second topic, we will discuss construction methods of elliptic curves over finite fields. The group of an elliptic curve over a finite field has a finite number of elements which we call points. The finite number of elements is called the order of the elliptic curve. The result of a curve construction method will be the curve itself, i.e. parameters of the curve and its order. We will discuss three types of construction methods for elliptic curves over finite fields. These are:

1. Generate a random elliptic curve over a finite field and count the points on its group structure, in short the generating-and-point-counting-method.

2. Construct an elliptic curve over a finite field with complex multiplication, in short the *CM-method* or Atkin-Morain approach.

3. Construct an elliptic curve over a finite field with a prescribed order, which is considered as an extension of the CM-method.

The first and third method will be introduced conceptually and rudimentarily implemented as a proof of concept. The second method will be the core subject of the second topic. The CM-method introduced by A.O.L Atkin use a fair amount of abstract theory and the algorithms for the implementation are sophisticated. Therefore, for the implementation of the CM-method, we will use the *bottom-up* strategy. That is, we first introduce and implement the data structures and algorithms of identifiable topics of CM-method like

- fundamental discriminant,
- modified Cornachia algorithm,
- binary quadratic forms,
- class number computation,
- Hilbert class polynomial

and then piece these topics together to implement the CM-method.

In the third topic, we will use the results from topic one and two and deploy those to prove the primality of a given integer. Primality proving algorithms based on elliptic curves are called elliptic curve primality proving (ECPP). Here, we will explain and develop the two ECPP algorithms:

- Goldwasser-Kilian's ECPP and
- Atkin-Morain's ECPP

2

Every primality proving process results in a certificate. A certificate enables us to repeat the proof without repeating the complete ECPP algorithm. That is, the proof can be repeated by checking the certificate by a program written by any other user. Finally, we will compare the run-time behaviour of the two elliptic curve types with respect to Atkin-Morain's ECPP.

Each of these three topics lead to algorithms that are based on mathematical definitions, propositions, theorems, etc. and are discussed in many different articles. In these articles, the resulting algorithms are mostly given as pseudocode. In this master thesis, we choose a more practical approach and develop the algorithms in Java as needed by using all the advantages of object-oriented development. That is, the development process will be well documented and the resulting algorithms and data structures are short, easy to read and extensible. Therefore, instead of using pseudocodes, we immediately present the source code as a description of the algorithms.

Chapter 2.

Elliptic curves

An elliptic curve E is a graph of the equation $y^2 = x^3 + ax + b$, where a, b, x and y are from any field K with the condition $4a^3 + 27b^2 \neq 0$. The values a, b are constants and are called the parameters or the coefficients of the elliptic curve.

Elliptic curves of the form $y^2 = x^3 + ax + b$ are called *short Weierstraß form* or just *Weierstraß form*. Other forms of equations which are also elliptic curves are *twisted Edwards* curves, *inverted Edwards* curves or the *Montgomery* curves, etc.

The variables x and y, that satisfy the Weierstraß equation are called *points* and are denoted by 2-tuples (x, y). The set of all K-rational points on E is given by the expression $E(K) = \{(x, y) \in K \times K : y^2 = x^3 + ax + b\}$.

The most unexpected property of elliptic curves defined over an arbitrary field K is the existence of a natural group operation on the set $E(K)$. With this property elliptic curves become interesting not only in their own right, but also for cryptography and primality proving.

The first purpose of this chapter is to give some background information about arithmetical properties of an elliptic curve. The second purpose is to discuss Hasse's theorem which plays a major role for elliptic curves over finite fields. Finally, the third purpose is to develop an *elliptic curve arithmetic system*, so that we can do arithmetical operations on elliptic curves.

The content of the first three sections is mainly based on [27][1] and [2][2]. The description of Hasse's theorem is based on [30]. Besides the section about twisted Edwards curve, most of the algorithms are from [4] and [5] and will be implemented in Java programming language.

2.1. Weierstraß equations

From the perspective of *algebraic geometry* an elliptic curve is an abelian variety defined by

Definition 2.1.1. *An elliptic curve over K is a pair (E, O), where E is a curve over K of genus one and $O \in E$, often just written as E.*

---

[1] Chapter III, The Geometry of Elliptic Curves (page 45-109).
[2] Chapter III, Cubic Curves in Weierstrass Form (page 50-79).

This definition is quite abstract, but it is a good starting point to explain the terminology. At the end of this section, we will give a more practical definition.

An elliptic curve defined as above is given by explicit polynomial equations. Geometrically, if we take the field of complex numbers, an elliptic curve is a type of cubic curve whose solutions are confined to a region of space that is topologically equivalent to a torus. Actually, this is the meaning of genus one. Just to compare with, a genus zero surface is a sphere. As mentioned, there exists a natural group operation on $E(K)$ and O represents the identity element on that group.

Every elliptic curve can be written as the locus in a projective plane[3] $\mathbb{P}^2_K$ of a cubic equation with only one point on the line ∞. This is given by the standard generalized form with homogeneous coordinates

$$Y^2Z + a_1XYZ + a_3YZ^2 = X^3 + a_2X^2Z + a_4XZ^2 + a_6Z^3 \tag{2.1}$$

where $O = (0,1,0)$ is the identity and $a_1, a_3, a_2, a_4, a_6 \in K$.

By using non-homogeneous coordinates $x = \frac{X}{Z}$ and $y = \frac{Y}{Z}$ with $Z \neq 0$ we get the Weierstraß equation[4] in affine plane, always remembering that there is the extra point $O = (0,1,0)$ out at infinity.

$$E : y^2 + a_1xy + a_3y = x^3 + a_2x^2 + a_4x + a_6 \tag{2.2}$$

where $a_1, a_3, a_2, a_4, a_6 \in K$. Then E is said to be *defined over* K.

For $char(K) \neq 2$ we simplfy the equation by replacing $y + \frac{1}{2}(a_1x + a_3)$ by $\frac{1}{2}y$. This gives an equation of the form

$$E : y^2 = 4x^3 + b_2x^2 + 2b_4x + b_6 \tag{2.3}$$

where

$$
\begin{aligned}
b_2 &= a_1^2 + 4a_2, \\
b_4 &= 2a_4 + a_1a_3, \\
b_6 &= a_3^2 + 4a_6.
\end{aligned}
$$

Further standard definitions are

$$
\begin{aligned}
c_4 &= b_2^2 - 24b_4, \\
c_6 &= -b_2^3 + 36b_2b_4 - 216b_6.
\end{aligned}
$$

The next simplification assumes $char(K) \neq 2,3$. By replacing (x,y) in 2.3 with $(\frac{x-3b_2}{36}, \frac{y}{108})$, the term x^2 will be eliminated, so that we get the simpler equation

---

[3]See [26], Appendix A, Projective Geometry.
[4]We call it Weierstraß equation, because a Weierstraß curve is implicitly also an elliptic curve. A Weierstraß equation becomes an elliptic curve with some additional conditions.

$$E : y^2 = x^3 - 27c_4 x - 54c_6. \tag{2.4}$$

Now, we will generalize this result and call the equation

$$E : y^2 = x^3 + ax + b \tag{2.5}$$

the *short form* of Weierstraß equation, where a, b, are rational constants from any field K and x, y are rationals.

2.1.1. Discriminant Δ and j-invariant

The discriminant Δ of the curve will help to classify curves given by the Weierstraß equation. For that we define

$$\begin{aligned} b_8 &= a_1^2 a_6 + 4a_2 a_6 - a_1 a_3 a_4 + a_2 a_3^2 - a_4^2, \\ \Delta &= -b_2^2 b_8 - 8b_4^3 - 27b_6^2 + 9b_2 b_4 b_6 \\ &= \frac{c_4^3 - c_6^2}{1728}. \end{aligned}$$

Finally, we express the term Δ with a and b from the Equation 2.5, then we get the relation

$$\Delta = \frac{1}{108^4}(4a^3 + 27b^2). \tag{2.6}$$

Another important quantity of elliptic curves is the j-invariant.The definition of j-invariant is given by

$$j = \frac{c_4^3}{\Delta}.$$

The j-invariant can also be expressed by the coefficient a, b of equation 2.5.

$$j = 1728\frac{4a^3}{4a^3 + 27b^2}. \tag{2.7}$$

Two elliptic curves are isomorphic over $\bar{K}$ if and only if they have the same j-invariant. This is a very important fact about elliptic curves and the prove is given in [27] pages 51-52.

If $j \neq 0, 1728$, then the elliptic curve can be expressed with

$$y^2 = x^3 + \frac{3j}{1728 - j}x + \frac{2j}{1728 - j}. \tag{2.8}$$

If we know the value for j, we can construct a curve. Therefore, identifying j for a curve with some special properties will be the key concept for elliptic curve construction algorithm.

If two different elliptic curves over $\bar{K}$, but not over K, have the same j-invariant, then we say that the two curves are *twists* of each other. The unique twist of E is called the *quadratic twist*.

In the next chapter, we will implement an algorithm, that always generates two elliptic curves by using the same input values. The following theorem shows the dependencies of the one curve parameters from its twisted curve parameters.

Theorem 2.1.2. *Let* $y_1^2 = x_1^3 + a_1 x_1 + b_1$, $y_2^2 = x_2^3 + a_2 x_2 + b_2$ *be two elliptic curves with j-invariants j_1 and j_2, respectively. If $j_1 = j_2$, then there exists $g \neq 0 \in K$ such that*

$$a_2 = g^4 a_1, b_2 = g^6 b_1. \tag{2.9}$$

The transformation

$$x_2 = g^2 x_1, y_2 = g^3 y_1. \tag{2.10}$$

takes one equation to the other.

For the proof, see [30], page 46.

2.1.2. Classification of Weierstraß equations

The following three Weierstraß equations are examples of different type of classes of curves.

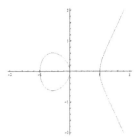

Figure 2.1.: Non-singular curve $y^2 = x^3 - x$ with $\Delta = 64$

Curves given by the Weierstraß equation can be classified as follows:

1. It is non-singular if and only if $\Delta \neq 0$

2. It has a node if and only if $\Delta = 0$ and $c_4 \neq 0$

3. It has a cusp if and only if $\Delta = c_4 = 0$

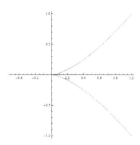

Figure 2.2.: Singular curve (cusp) $y^2 = x^3$ with $\Delta = 0$

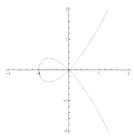

Figure 2.3.: Singular curve (node) $y^2 = x^3 + x$ with $\Delta = 0$

For elliptic curves, we expect a non-singular Weierstraß equation. Non-singularity of a Weierstraß equation is equivalent to the following statements:

1. The partial derivatives for E do not vanish simultaneously for any point (x, y) on the curve E.

2. The equation $x^3 + ax + b = 0$ has no multiple roots.

With all that information so far, we are able to give an appropriate and *practical* definition of an elliptic curve.

Definition 2.1.3. *A non-singular cubic curve*

$$E : y^2 = x^3 + ax + b \tag{2.11}$$

with $4a^3 + 27b^2 \neq 0$ and characteristic of K is not 2 or 3, and with coefficients a, b in a field K and with at least one point with coordinates in K (that are not all zero) is said to be an elliptic curve over K. We denote by $E(K)$ the set of points with coordinates in K that satisfy the equation together with the point at infinity, denoted by O.

$$E(K) = \{(x, y) \in K \times K : y^2 = x^3 + ax + b\} \cup \{O\} \tag{2.12}$$

2.2. Group law

By defining a binary operation on the set $E(K)$, the set $E(K)$ turns into an abelian group. We interpret the binary operation geometrically in terms of *chord-tangent composition law*. The group law algorithm enables us to do computations on elliptic curves, which can be implemented in an arbitrary programming language.

2.2.1. Composition law

If P and Q are two points on the elliptic curve, then we can uniquely describe a third point which is the intersection of the curve with the line through P and Q (Part 1 of Figure 2.4). If the line is tangent to the curve at a point, then that point is counted twice (Part 2 of Figure 2.4). If the line is parallel to the y-axis, we define the third point as the point at *infinity*, denoted O. There are again two cases which we have to consider (Part 3, 4 of Figure 2.4).

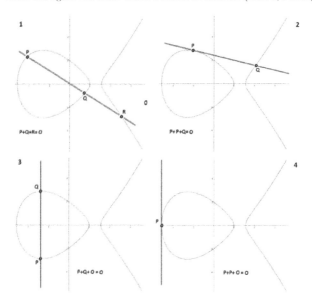

Figure 2.4.: Chord-tangent composition law

Exactly one of these conditions then holds for any pair of points on an elliptic curve. Resumed we get four equations for $P, Q, R \in E(K)$

9

$$
\begin{aligned}
P + Q + R &= O \\
P + P + Q &= O \\
P + Q + O &= O \\
P + P + O &= O
\end{aligned}
$$

The algebraic properties of the composition law is given by the following

Proposition 2.2.1. *The composition law has the following properties:*

1. *If a line L intersects E at the points P, Q, R, then $(P + Q) + R = O$.*

2. *$P + O = P$ for all $P \in E$.*

3. *$P + Q = Q + P$ for all $P, Q \in E$.*

4. *Let $P \in E$. There is a point of E, denoted $-P$, so that $P + (-P) = O$.*

5. *Let $P, Q, R \in E$. Then $(P + Q) + R = P + (Q + R)$.*

The composition law makes E into an abelian group with identity element O.

The proof can be found in [27], page 57.

Notice, the group law does not use any specialities of the Weierstraß equation. For the explanation and the proof it is sufficient to proceed with algebraic geometric lines. But for the group law algorithm, as described in the next section, we need the specialities of the Weierstraß equation.

2.2.2. Group law algorithm

Let E be an elliptic curve given by a Weierstraß equation[5] $E : y^2 = x^3 + ax + b$. Let $P_1 = (x_1, y_1)$ and $P_2 = (x_2, y_2)$ on E be given. A line through P_1 and P_2 results in a third intersection point P_3' on E.

By composition law, we get

$$
P_1 + P_2 + P_3' = O,
$$

and therefore (by setting $P_3 = -P_3'$)

$$
P_1 + P_2 = -P_3' = P_3.
$$

The coordinates of the resulting point P_3 on E is given by reflection of point P_3' across the x-axis (see Figure 2.5).

---

[5]The derivation of the formulas based on Weierstraß equation $E : y^2 + a_1 xy + a_3 y = x^3 + a_2 x^2 + a_4 x + a_6$ can be found in [2]. Here, we are using the Weierstraß equation in short form.

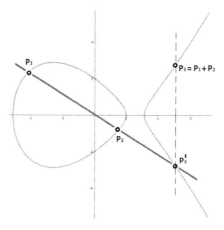

Figure 2.5.: Computing the coordinates of the third point

With some computations, we get the formulas for the third point.

$$y = mx + n = \begin{cases} \text{line } M \text{ through } P_1 \text{ and } P_2 & \text{if } P_1 \neq P_2 \text{ (chord case)} \\ \text{tangent line } M \text{ at } P_1 & \text{if } P_1 = P_2 \text{ (tangent case).} \end{cases}$$

The formulas for m and n in the chord case are formulas for the line through P_1 and P_2. In the tangent case, we compute $m = \frac{dy}{dx}$ by implicit differentiation. The result is

$$m = \begin{cases} \frac{y_2 - y_1}{x_2 - x_1} & \text{(in chord case)} \\ \frac{3x_1^2 + a}{2y_1} & \text{(in tangent case),} \end{cases} \tag{2.13}$$

$$n = y_1 - mx_1 = y_2 - mx_2. \tag{2.14}$$

By setting $y^2 = (mx + n)^2 = x^3 + ax + b$, we get the final result for the coordinates of the third point.

$$P_1 + P_2 = \begin{cases} O, & \text{if } P_1 = -P_2 \\ (m^2 - x_1 - x_2, m(x_1 - x_3) - y_1), & \text{else.} \end{cases} \tag{2.15}$$

2.2.3. Operations based on group law algorithm

Operations based on group law algorithm can be derived from the addition operation as introduced in last section. Let P be a point on a elliptic curve E. By adding P to itself with

Formula 2.15, we get the *double* operation. Notice, the Java method name of this operation will be *duplicate*, since *double* is a keyword in Java.

Let P, Q be points on a elliptic curve E with $P + Q = O$. Then we get $P = -Q$ and the negative coordinates of the point $P = (x, y)$ is given by the coordinates $(x, -y)$. This operation will be implemented by the method *negate*.

Subtracting two points is adding the first point P on E to the negated second point Q on E. This operation will be implemented by the method *subtract*.

Multiplying a point P on E with a positive integer k is to add k-times P to itself. This is the interpretation of the operation *multiply*. An efficient implementation of multiply operation is realized with a *addition-subtraction-ladder* in Section 2.5.2.3.

For details about elliptic curve arithmetic see [5] Section 7.2.

2.3. Abstract group structure of elliptic curves over some fixed fields

An essential part of elliptic curve theory is the research of the abstract group structure of $E(K)$, where K is an arbitrary field. Depending on the underlying field K the elliptic curve *looks* different, i.e. the group structure of the elliptic curve is different. In this section, we discuss the group structure of $E(K)$ where K is $\mathbb{R}$, $\mathbb{C}$ or $\mathbb{Q}$. We discuss the group structure of $E(K)$ where K is a finite field. Since finite fields are important for doing practical arithmetics on elliptic curves, the next section will be completely dedicated to elliptic curves over finite field.

The following definitions will be used in this sections.

Definition 2.3.1. *Finite/infinite order of an element P. An element P of any group is said to have order m if*
$$mP = O, \tag{2.16}$$
but $m'P \neq O$ for all integers $1 \leq m' \leq m$. If such an m exists, then P has finite order; otherwise it has infinite order.

Definition 2.3.2. *Circle group. The circle group, denoted by S^1, is the multiplicative group of all complex numbers with absolute value 1, i.e., the unit circle in the complex plane.*
$$S^1 = \{z \in \mathbb{C} : |z| = 1\}. \tag{2.17}$$
For each integer m, the points of finite order dividing m form a cyclic group of order m.

Definition 2.3.3. *Torsion subgroup. In any group, there is a main distinction between elements of finite order and elements of infinite order. In an abelian group, the set of elements of finite order form a subgroup, called the torsion subgroup.*

2.3.1. Elliptic curves over $\mathbb{R}$

If the elliptic curve has one real root, the real points form one component, illustrated in Figure 2.6.

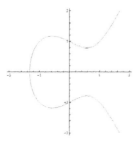

Figure 2.6.: One real component $y^2 = x^3 - x + 1$

Then $E(\mathbb{R})$ is isomorphic to a circle group.

$$E(\mathbb{R}) \cong S^1. \tag{2.18}$$

If the elliptic curve has three real roots, the real points form two components, illustrated in Figure 2.7.

Figure 2.7.: Two connected components $y^2 = x^3 - 2x + 1$

Then $E(\mathbb{R})$ is isomorphic to product of circle group with a group of order two[6].

$$E(\mathbb{R}) \cong S^1 \times G_2. \tag{2.19}$$

---

[6]For more explanation see [26], page 42.

2.3.2. Elliptic curves over $\mathbb{C}$

To explain elliptic curves over $\mathbb{C}$, we need to explain the terms *lattice* and *fundamental discriminant* first. For a detailed treatment of the subject in this section see [2], [30] and [16].

Let ω_1, ω_2 be complex numbers that are linearly independent over $\mathbb{R}$. Without loss of generality we may assume that $Im(\frac{\omega_2}{\omega_1}) > 0$, then this requirement is satisfied.

Then the lattice L generated by ω_1, ω_2 is defined as

$$L = \mathbb{Z}\omega_1 + \mathbb{Z}\omega_2 = \{m\omega_1 + n\omega_2 \mid m, n \in \mathbb{Z}\}. \tag{2.20}$$

In short we write $L = [\omega 1, \omega 2]$ and illustrate the lattice L as a regularly spaced array of points in $\mathbb{C}$. Figure 2.8 is an illustration of a lattice.

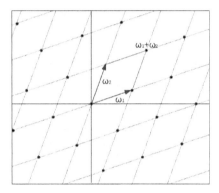

Figure 2.8.: Lattice in a complex plane

Associated with each lattice is a fundamental parallelogram Λ. The fundamental parallelogram Λ for lattice L is defined as

$$\Lambda = \{a\omega_1 + b\omega_2 \mid 0 \leq a \leq 1, 0 \leq b \leq 1\}. \tag{2.21}$$

Figure 2.9 is an illustration of a fundamental parallelogram.

We can generate the lattice L by translating the verticies of Λ in any integral linear combination of ω_1 and ω_2.

Let $\mathbb{C}/L$ denote the quotient of the additive group of complex numbers by the lattice L and we can think of the fundamental parallelogram Λ as a representative of the set $\mathbb{C}/L$. Using Λ as a representant of $\mathbb{C}/L$, we can identify the opposite sides of the parallelogram. By gluing the opposite sites we get a torus like illustrated in Figure 2.10

14

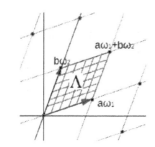

Figure 2.9.: Fundamental parallelogram

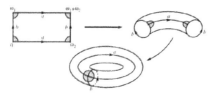

Figure 2.10.: Torus

Functions defined over $\mathbb{C}/L$ which are meromorphic[7] and doubly periodic are called *elliptic functions*.

The criteria that a function f is double periodic is given by

$$f(z + \omega_i) = f(z) \text{ with } z \in \mathbb{C} \text{ and } i \in \{1, 2\}. \tag{2.22}$$

Let L be a given lattice with its generating ω_1 and ω_2. Then ω_1 and ω_2 are the two periods of the elliptic function, hence the name doubly periodic.

The most important example of an elliptic function in $\mathbb{C}$ is the Weierstraß $\wp$-function which is defined with respect to L.

$$\wp(z) = \wp(z; L) = \begin{cases} \frac{1}{z^2} + \sum_{\omega \in L \setminus \{0\}} \left[\frac{1}{(z-\omega)^2} - \frac{1}{\omega^2} \right] & , z \notin L \\ \infty & , z \in L \end{cases} \tag{2.23}$$

It can be shown[8], that $\wp(z)$ satisfies the differential equation

---

[7] Complex differentiable function in a neighborhood of every point in its domain except a set of isolated points. For details see [16].

[8] See [19] for the proof.

$$\wp'(z)^2 = 4\wp(z)^3 - g_2\wp(z) - g_3, \tag{2.24}$$

where the coefficients are expressible in terms of the periods. That is

$$g_2 = 60G_4 \text{ and } g_3 = 140G_6 \text{ where } G_k = \sum_{\omega \in L \setminus \{0\}} \frac{1}{\omega^k}.$$

The main result of this short section is that there is an isomorphic relationship between $\mathbb{C}/L$ and $E(\mathbb{C})$. This is guarenteed by the following

Theorem 2.3.4. *Let L be a lattice on $\mathbb{C}$ and E be the elliptic curve $y^2 = 4x^3 - g_2x - g_3$. Then the map φ defined by*

$$
\begin{aligned}
\varphi : \mathbb{C}/L &\rightarrow E(\mathbb{C}) \\
z &\rightarrow (\wp(z), \wp'(z)) \\
0 &\rightarrow \infty
\end{aligned}
$$

is a group isomorphism under addition modulo L in $\mathbb{C}/L$ and standard elliptic curve operation in $E(\mathbb{C})$.

For the proof, see [30], page 270.

We repeat, as an abstract group, the group $E(\mathbb{C})$ is isomorphic to $\mathbb{C}/L$.

$$E(\mathbb{C}) \cong \mathbb{C}/L. \tag{2.25}$$

Since $\wp$ is doubly periodic function, it generalizes the classical function e^z that has the single period $2\pi i$. Hence, we can extend the description of the abstract group to

$$E(\mathbb{C}) \cong \mathbb{C}/L \cong S^1 \times S^1. \tag{2.26}$$

2.3.3. Elliptic curves over $\mathbb{Q}$

The group of rational points $E(\mathbb{Q})$ is a subgroup of the group of real points $E(\mathbb{R})$. *Mordell's* theorem describes the structure of $E(\mathbb{Q})$. The advanced proof can be found in [26], Chapter 3.

Theorem 2.3.5. *Let E be an elliptic curve given by the equation*

$$E : y^2 = x^3 + ax + b \text{ with } a, b \in \mathbb{Q}. \tag{2.27}$$

Then the group of rational points $E(\mathbb{Q})$ is a finitely generated abelian group. There is a finite set of points $P_1 \cdots P_t \in E(\mathbb{Q})$ so that every point $P \in E(\mathbb{Q})$ can be written in the form

$$P = n_1P_1 + n_2P_2 + \cdots + n_tP_t \text{ for some } n_1, n_2, \cdots, n_t \in \mathbb{Z}. \tag{2.28}$$

The expression $n_i P_i$ with $i = 1, 2, ..., t$ is n_i-times multiplication of the point P_i with itself like described in section 2.2.3.

It follows from the fundamental theorem on abelian groups that $E(\mathbb{Q})$, as an abstract group, is isomorphic to a direct sum of infinite cyclic groups and finite cyclic groups. That is

$$E(\mathbb{Q}) \cong E(\mathbb{Q})_{tors} \times \underbrace{\mathbb{Z} \times \mathbb{Z} \times \cdots \times \mathbb{Z}}_{r \text{ copies}}. \tag{2.29}$$

$E(\mathbb{Q})_{tors}$ is the torsion subgroup from Definition 2.3.3. The integer r is called the *rank* of $E(\mathbb{Q})$.

2.4. Elliptic curves over $\mathbb{F}_q$ and Hasse's theorem

Since finite fields are also fields, everything stated in the last sections will also be valid for finite fields. Let $\mathbb{F}_q$ be a finite field, where q is a prime power, i.e. $q = p^k$ with p prime and $k \in \mathbb{N}$. Let E be an elliptic curve defined over $\mathbb{F}_q$. Then the *order* $\#E(\mathbb{F}_q)$ denotes the number of points in the group $E(\mathbb{F}_q)$. We also assume for $a, b \in \mathbb{F}_q$, that q is not dividing $4a^3 + 27b^2$. This condition ensures that the curve is non-singular.

An estimation for $\#E(\mathbb{F}_q)$ is given by *Helmut Hasse* in the 1930's. Hasse's theorem is considered as the main theorem concerning elliptic curves over finite fields. We will give a proof of Hasse's theorem in this section. The proof is oriented on [30], but the needed lemmas and propositions are more consecutively. The synopsis of the proof will cover essential topics with respect to elliptic curves over finite fields.

2.4.1. Hasse's theorem

Based on Hasse's theorem, the order of the group $E(\mathbb{F}_q)$ is an integer in the Hasse interval $[q + 1 - 2\sqrt{q}, q + 1 + 2\sqrt{q}]$ around $q + 1$. This theorem which is the main theorem concerning elliptic curves over finite fields, is given as follows:

Theorem 2.4.1. *Let E be an elliptic curve over the finite field $\mathbb{F}_q$. Then*

$$|\#E(\mathbb{F}_q) - q - 1| \leq 2\sqrt{q}. \tag{2.30}$$

To understand the proof of Hasse's theorem, we have to discuss maps between elliptic curves. The next section introduces isogenies which are homomorphisms between elliptic curves.

2.4.2. Isogenies

In the theory of elliptic curves isogenies allow us to relate one elliptic curve to another. The following is the definition of isogeny.

Definition 2.4.2. *Let E_1 and E_2 be elliptic curves. An isogeny between E_1 and E_2 is a morphism*

$$\phi : E_1 \rightarrow E_2 \tag{2.31}$$

satisfying $\phi(O) = O$. E_1 and E_2 are isogenous if there is an isogeny ϕ between them with $\phi(E_1) \neq \{O\}$.

In fact an isogeny between two elliptic curves E_1 and E_2 maps the given point on E_1 to that on E_2. Only the identity element O has to be preserved during the mapping, that is what $\phi(O) = O$ means.

With isogeny, we can introduce different morphisms between elliptic curves. Thus let

$$Hom(E_1, E_2) = \{ \text{ isogenies } \phi : E_1 \rightarrow E_2 \} . \tag{2.32}$$

Let $\phi, \psi \in Hom(E_1, E_2)$ and P is a point on E_1. Then $Hom(E_1, E_2)$ is a group under addition law

$$(\phi + \psi)(P) = \phi(P) + \psi(P). \tag{2.33}$$

If $E_1 = E_2$, then we can also compose isogenies. Thus if E is an elliptic curve, we let

$$End(E) = Hom(E, E). \tag{2.34}$$

be the ring with addition as above and multiplication given by composition,

$$(\phi\psi)(P) = \phi(\psi(P)). \tag{2.35}$$

$End(E)$ is called the *endomorphism ring* of E. The endomorphism ring of an elliptic curve is an important invariant, which will also appear in the theory of *complex multiplication*. The invertible elements of $End(E)$ form the *automorphism group* of E, which is denoted $Aut(E)$.

If E_1, E_2, E are defined over a field K, then we can restrict attention to those isogenies defined over K. The corresponding groups of isogenies are denoted with $Hom(E_1(K), E_2(K))$, $End(E(K))$, $Aut(E(K))$.

2.4.3. Frobenius map

An example of an endomorphism is the *Frobenius* map, which is used in the proof of Hasse's theorem.

Definition 2.4.3. *Let $\mathbb{F}_q$ be a finite field with an algebraic closure $\bar{\mathbb{F}}_q$. The Frobenius map is the map*

$$\phi_q : \bar{\mathbb{F}}_q \to \bar{\mathbb{F}}_q \text{ defined by } \phi_q(x) = x^q. \tag{2.36}$$

On elliptic curves we have $\phi_q(x, y) = (x^q, y^q)$ and $\phi_q(O) = O$.

2.4.4. Preliminaries for the proof of Hasse's theorem

We start with the definition of the terms *separable/inseparable* polynomial, which comes from distinctness of the roots of a polynomial.

Definition 2.4.4. *A non-zero polynomial $f(X) \in K[X]$ is called separable when it has distinct roots in a splitting field over K. That is, each root of $f(X)$ has multiplicity 1. If $f(X)$ has a multiple root then $f(X)$ is called inseparable.*

There is an easy analytic way to check if a given polynomial is separable. The following theorem gives a criterion for separability, where the proof can be found in [11].

Theorem 2.4.5. *A non-zero polynomial in $K[X]$ is separable if and only if it is relatively prime to its derivative in $K[X]$.*

A trivial corollary, which follows from this theorem is given as follows.

Corollary 2.4.6. *If the derivative of a non-zero polynomial in $K[X]$ is zero, then the polynomial is inseparable.*

The next lemma predicates some basic property of the Frobenius map.

Lemma 2.4.7. *Let E be an elliptic curve defined over $\mathbb{F}_q$ and ϕ_q a Frobenius map. Then we have the following statements.*

1. ϕ_q is an endomorphism of E of degree q.

2. ϕ_q is inseparable.

The proof is given in [30], page 53. The second part is also easy to argue with Corollary 2.4.6. Since $q = 0$ in $\mathbb{F}_q$, the derivative of the non-zero polynomial x^q is zero, hence ϕ_q is inseparable.

The next proposition gives a relationship between the degree and the kernel[9] of endomorphism of an elliptic curve. Separability plays again an important role.

---

[9]The kernel of $\alpha \in End(E)$ is defined as $ker(\alpha) = \{(x, y) \in E \mid \alpha : E \to E, \alpha(x, y) = O\}$

Proposition 2.4.8. *Let $\alpha \neq 0$ be a separable endomorphism of an elliptic curve E. Then*

$$deg(\alpha) = \#ker(\alpha) \tag{2.37}$$

where $ker(\alpha)$ is the kernel of the homomorphism $\alpha : E(\bar{\mathbb{F}}_q) \to E(\bar{\mathbb{F}}_q)$. If $\alpha \neq 0$ is inseparable, then

$$deg(\alpha) > \#ker(\alpha) \tag{2.38}$$

The proof is in [30], page 54.

The next lemma enables a relationship between the Frobenius endomorphism and elements of $E(\mathbb{F}_q)$.

Lemma 2.4.9. *Let E be defined over $\mathbb{F}_q$ and let $(x, y) \in E(\bar{\mathbb{F}}_q)$.*

1. *$\phi_q(x, y) \in E(\bar{\mathbb{F}}_q)$.*

2. *$(x, y) \in E(\mathbb{F}_q)$ if and only if $\phi_q(x, y) = (x, y)$.*

The proof is in [30], page 99.

The next proposition is the key to counting points on elliptic curves and therefore crucial for the proof of Hasse's theorem.

Proposition 2.4.10. *Let E be defined over $\mathbb{F}_q$ and let $n \geq 1$.*

1. *$ker(\phi_q^n - 1) = E(\mathbb{F}_{q^n})$.*

2. *$\phi_q^n - 1$ is a separable endomorphism, so $\#E(\mathbb{F}_{q^n}) = deg(\phi_q^n - 1)$.*

Proof. Part 1 of Proposition 2.4.10. Note $\phi_q^n = \phi_{q^n}$. Considering $\phi_q^2 = (x^q)^q = x^{q \cdot q} = x^{q^2}$ for the quadratic case. By extending this to n, we get $\phi_q^n(x) = x^{q^n}$, therefore $\phi_q^n = (x^{q^n}, y^{q^n}) = \phi_{q^n}$. Now we restate part 2 of Lemma 2.4.9. Let $P = (x, y) \in E$. Then

$$
\begin{aligned}
\phi_q^n(P) = \phi_{q^n}(P) &= P, \\
\phi_{q^n}(P) - P &= O, \\
(\phi_{q^n} - 1)(P) &= O, \\
ker(\phi_{q^n} - 1) &= E(\mathbb{F}_{q^n}). \tag{2.39}
\end{aligned}
$$

$\square$

For part 2 of the proof, we need a further proposition.

Proposition 2.4.11. *Let E be defined over $\mathbb{F}_q$. Let r and s be integers, not both 0. The endomorphism $r\phi_q + s$ is separable if and only if $p \nmid s$.*

The proof is in [30], page 58/59.

Proof. *Part 2 of Proposition 2.4.10.* $\phi_q^n = \phi_q \circ \phi_q \circ \cdots \circ \phi_q$ is a composition of endomorphisms, hence an endomorphism. Multiplication by -1 is an endomorphism. Therefore the sum $\phi_q^n - 1$ is a endomorphism. Separability follows from Proposition 2.4.11 ($r = 1, s = -1$ and obviously $p \nmid -1$) and with Proposition 2.4.8 we have the desired result. $\qquad\square$

Another proposition will be necessary as preparation for the proof of Hasse's theorem.

Proposition 2.4.12. *Let E be defined over $\mathbb{F}_q$ and α and β be endomorphisms on E and let a and b be integers. The endomorphism $a\alpha + b\beta$ is defined by*

$$(a\alpha + b\beta)(P) = a\alpha(P) + b\beta(P). \tag{2.40}$$

Then we have

$$deg(a\alpha + b\beta) = a^2 deg(\alpha) + b^2 deg(\beta) + ab(deg(\alpha + \beta) - deg(\alpha) - deg(\beta)). \tag{2.41}$$

The proof is in [30], page 90.

We define a variable t, which denotes a term from Hasse's theorem, as

$$t = q + 1 - \#E(\mathbb{F}_q). \tag{2.42}$$

The following lemma is then additionally expressed with t and q.

Lemma 2.4.13. *Let r, s be integers with $gcd(s,q) = 1$. Then*

$$deg(r\phi_q - s) = r^2 q + s^2 - rst. \tag{2.43}$$

Proof. With Proposition 2.4.10 we have

$$\begin{aligned} t &= q + 1 - \#E(\mathbb{F}_q), \\ &= q + 1 - deg(\phi_q - 1). \end{aligned}$$

With Proposition 2.4.12 and

$$\begin{aligned} deg(\phi_q) &= q, \\ deg(-1) &= 1, \end{aligned}$$

we conclude

$$\begin{aligned} deg(r\phi_q - s) &= r^2 deg(\phi_q) + s^2 deg(-1) + rs(deg(\phi_q - 1) - deg(\phi_q) - deg(-1)) \\ &= r^2 q + s^2 + rs(deg(\phi_q - 1) - q - 1) \\ &= r^2 q + s^2 - rst. \end{aligned}$$

$\qquad\square$

With this preliminaries, we are ready to prove Hasse's theorem.

2.4.5. Proof of Hasse's theorem

Let E be an elliptic curve over a finite field $\mathbb{F}_q$. Hasse's theorem bounds the number of points on E. For $t = q + 1 - \#E(\mathbb{F}_q)$, we get $|t| \leq 2\sqrt{q}$.

Proof. Hasse's theorem. A degree of a endomorphism can't be negative, hence the Lemma 2.4.13 implies
$$0 \leq deg(r\phi_q - s) = r^2 q + s^2 - rst.$$

We multiply the inequality with $\frac{1}{s^2}$ (remember $gcd(s,q) = 1$) and get
$$0 \leq q(\frac{r}{s})^2 - t(\frac{r}{s}) + 1.$$

The set $\{\frac{r}{s} \mid gcd(s,q) = 1\}$ is dense in $\mathbb{R}$. Therefore we may consider the term $qx^2 - tx + 1$ with $x \in \mathbb{R}$, which has its minimum for $2qx - t = 0$. By plug in $x = \frac{t}{2q}$ into the term, we get

$$0 \leq q \left(\frac{t}{2q}\right)^2 - t\frac{t}{2q} + 1 = -\frac{t^2}{4q} + 1.$$

That is

$$
\begin{aligned}
t^2 - 4q &\leq 0 \\
|t| &\leq 2\sqrt{q}.
\end{aligned}
$$

This completes the proof of Hasse's theorem.

$\square$

2.4.6. Group structure of elliptic curves over $\mathbb{F}_q$

An elliptic curve over finite field $\mathbb{F}_q$ has finitely many pairs (x,y) with $x, y \in \mathbb{F}_q$. With Hasse's theorem we know the group $E(\mathbb{F}_q)$ is also finite. An interesting question that arises is, what kind of algebraic group structure is on $E(\mathbb{F}_q)$?

To give a simplified answer to this question, we start with *Lagrange's* corollary which follows from *Lagrange's* theorem.

Theorem 2.4.14. *The order of a subgroup of a finite group is a divisor of the order of the group.*

Corollary 2.4.15. *Let G be a finite group with $\#G = n$ and e the identity in G. Then $a^n = e$ for all $a \in G$.*

The proofs are in [7], Section 1.2.

Hence, for elliptic curves over finite field $\mathbb{F}_q$, we have then

$$E(\mathbb{F}_q) \cong \mathbb{Z}_n \text{ or } E(\mathbb{F}_q) \cong \mathbb{Z}_{n_1} \times \mathbb{Z}_{n_2} \tag{2.44}$$

for some integer $n \geq 1$, or for some integers $n_1, n_2 \geq 1$ with n_1 dividing n_2.

2.4.7. An example of $E(\mathbb{F}_q)$

Let $E : y^2 = x^3 + x + 1$ be an elliptic curve over $\mathbb{F}_5$. Before identifying all the point on $E(\mathbb{F}_5)$, we identify the Hasse interval.

$$[5 + 1 - 2\sqrt{5} \approx 1.5, 5 + 1 + 2\sqrt{5} \approx 10.5] = [1.5, 10.5] \tag{2.45}$$

All the rational points are computed by plugging in the elements of $\mathbb{F}_5 = \{0, 1, 2, 3, 4\}$ into the polynomial $x^3 + x + 1$. Then we get by reduction modulo 5

$$
\begin{aligned}
x &= 0, \, y^2 = 0^3 + 0 + 1 = 1 \Rightarrow y = \pm 1 \\
x &= 1, \, y^2 = 1^3 + 1 + 1 = 3 \Rightarrow \text{ no solution} \\
x &= 2, \, y^2 = 2^3 + 2 + 1 = 11 \pmod 5 = 1 \Rightarrow y = \pm 1 \\
x &= 3, \, y^2 = 3^3 + 3 + 1 = 31 \pmod 5 = 1 \Rightarrow y = \pm 1 \\
x &= 4, \, y^2 = 4^3 + 4 + 1 = 64 \pmod 5 = 4 \Rightarrow y = \pm 2
\end{aligned}
$$

By considering the point at infinity, i.e. the neutral element, we get the set

$$
\begin{aligned}
E(\mathbb{F}_5) &= \{O, (0, \pm 1), (2, \pm 1), (3, \pm 1), (4, \pm 2)\} \\
&= \{O, (0, 1), (0, 4), (2, 1), (2, 4), (3, 1), (3, 4), (4, 2), (4, 3)\}
\end{aligned}
$$

The set $E(\mathbb{F}_5)$ forms an abelian group of order nine and the operation on $E(\mathbb{F}_5)$ is the well known point addition on elliptic curves. Indeed, the group table, illustrated in Table 2.1 shows this fact.

Figure 2.11 contains a plot of the points of $y^2 = x^3 + x + 1$ over the finite field $\mathbb{F}_5$, though note that the point at O is not explicitly drawn.

2.4.8. Bad and good reduction

For an elliptic curve over finite field $\mathbb{F}_q$ we can get a singular curve by reduction modulo q, if q divides the discriminant Δ of the elliptic curve. Then the discriminant Δ of the elliptic curve becomes zero. We say E over $\mathbb{F}_q$ has *bad reduction*, if Δ becomes zero by reduction modulo q. If E over $\mathbb{F}_q$ is non-singular by reduction modulo q, we say E has *good reduction* modulo q.

	O	(0,1)	(0,4)	(2,1)	(2,4)	(3,1)	(3,4)	(4,2)	(4,3)
O	O	(0,1)	(0,4)	(2,1)	(2,4)	(3,1)	(3,4)	(4,2)	(4,3)
(0,1)	(0,1)	(4,2)	O	(3,4)	(4,3)	(2,4)	(3,1)	(2,1)	(0,4)
(0,4)	(0,4)	O	(4,3)	(4,2)	(3,1)	(3,4)	(2,1)	(0,1)	(2,4)
(2,1)	(2,1)	(3,4)	(4,2)	(2,4)	O	(0,4)	(4,3)	(3,1)	(0,1)
(2,4)	(2,4)	(4,3)	(3,1)	O	(2,1)	(4,2)	(0,1)	(0,4)	(3,4)
(3,1)	(3,1)	(2,4)	(3,4)	(0,4)	(4,2)	(0,1)	O	(4,3)	(2,1)
(3,4)	(3,4)	(3,1)	(2,1)	(4,3)	(0,1)	O	(0,4)	(2,4)	(4,2)
(4,2)	(4,2)	(2,1)	(0,1)	(3,1)	(0,4)	(4,3)	(2,4)	(3,4)	O
(4,3)	(4,3)	(0,4)	(2,4)	(0,1)	(3,4)	(2,1)	(4,2)	O	(3,1)

Table 2.1.: Group Table $\mathbb{F}_5$ for $E : y^2 = x^3 + x + 1$

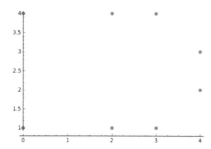

Figure 2.11.: Elliptic curve $y^2 = x^3 + x + 1$ over $\mathbb{F}_5$

2.5. Implementing the arithmetic of Weierstraß curve over finite fields

We startet introducing elliptic curves with the Weierstraß curve. This section will give a possible implementation of the arithmetic of Weierstraß curve and the essential parts of the source code will be listed in an outlined form. Because there are also other types of elliptic curves besides Weierstraß curve, we start with a general design of the software. In the next sections, we will also cover twisted Edwards curves.

2.5.1. Architectural perspective

The interface `EllipticCurveInterface` contains all the methods which will be necessary to do computation on elliptic curves. The `EllipticCurveInterface` has no restriction concerning the type of the elliptic curve and field whereupon the elliptic curve is defined. The only fixed datastructures are `BigInteger` and `Point`. `BigInteger` is a native Java class which allows arbitrary-precision integers operations[10].

```
1    public interface EllipticCurveInterface {
2    public Point getIdentity();
3    BigInteger discriminant();
4    BigInteger jInvariant();
5    public boolean isNonSingular();
6    public Point negate(Point p);
7    public Point subtract(Point p1, Point p2);
8    Point toAffineCoordinates(Point p);
9    public Point duplicate(Point p);
10   public Point add(Point p1, Point p2);
11   public Point multiply(Point p, BigInteger k);
12   }
```

Listing 2.1: Interface EllipticCurveInterface

`Point` is a simple *container class* which represents the projective coordinates of a point on an elliptic curve.

```
1  public class Point {
2    private BigInteger x;
3    private BigInteger y;
4    private BigInteger z;
5    public Point(BigInteger x, BigInteger y, BigInteger z) {
6      super();
7      this.x = x;
8      this.y = y;
9      this.z = z;
10   }
11   public BigInteger getX() { ..
12   public void setX(BigInteger x) { ..
13   public BigInteger getY() { ..
14   public void setY(BigInteger y) {..
15   public BigInteger getZ() {..
16   public void setZ(BigInteger z) {..
17 }
```

Listing 2.2: Class Point

`EllipticCurveBase` is an abstract implementation of the interface `EllipticCurveInterface`. This class has the attributes a and b which represents the parameters a and b of the elliptic curve. With this speciality, we are restricted to elliptic curves with two parameters like the short form of Weierstraß curve $y^2 = x^3 + ax + b$. The Listing 2.3 shows the outline of `EllipticCurveBase`.

```
1  public abstract class EllipticCurveBase implements EllipticCurveInterface {
2
3    protected BigInteger a;
4    protected BigInteger b;
5    protected BigInteger n;
```

---

[10]For details see javadoc for `java.math.BigInteger`

```
 6   public void init(BigInteger a, BigInteger b, BigInteger n) {
 7     this.a = a.mod(n);
 8     this.b = b.mod(n);
 9     this.n = n;
10   }
11   public BigInteger getN() {..
12   public void setN(BigInteger n) {..
13   public BigInteger getA() {..
14   public void setA(BigInteger a) {..
15   public BigInteger getB() {..
16   public void setB(BigInteger b) {..
17   public Point multiply(Point p, BigInteger k) {..
18 }
```

Listing 2.3: Class EllipticCurveBase

Multipliying[11] a given point P on an elliptic curve with an integer is an operation which is not depending on the choosen elliptic curve. This is why the method multiply is in EllipticCurveBase. We will explain this in the next section.

Until now there was no Weierstraß curve specific implementations. All the introduced classes may be also used for other elliptic curves that are represented by two parameters. However, the next classes will be Weierstraß curve specific and we will give a implementation for the affine[12] and the projective version. The Listing 2.4 shows the abstract class Weierstrass which extends the abstract class EllipticCurveBase and has methods that are independent from affine or projective version.

```
 1  /*
 2   * Based on Prime Numbers (Crandall/Pomerance) page 325
 3   */
 4  public abstract class Weierstrass extends EllipticCurveBase {
 5    /*
 6     * y^2=x^3+ax+b
 7     * Identity: (0:1:0)
 8     */
 9    private final Point IDENTITY = new Point(Const.ZERO, Const.ONE, Const.ZERO);
10    public Point getIdentity() {..
11    public BigInteger discriminant() {..
12    public BigInteger jInvariant() {..
13    public boolean isNonSingular() {..
14    public Point negate(Point p) {..
15    public Point subtract(Point p1, Point p2) {..
16  }
```

Listing 2.4: Class Weierstrass

The WeierstrassAffine class extends the abstract Weierstrass class and implements the three missing methods from EllipticCurveInterface.That means, the three methods are depending on the choosen coordinate system. For the method toAffineCoordinates the input and output is the same.

---

[11]See Section 2.2.3.
[12]The affine version is only for testing purposes

```
1  /*
2   * Based on Prime Numbers (Crandall/Pomerance) page 325
3   */
4  public class WeierstrassAffine extends Weierstrass {
5    public Point duplicate(Point p) {..
6    public Point add(Point p1, Point p2) {..
7    public Point toAffineCoordinates(Point p) {..
8  }
```

Listing 2.5: Class WeierstrassAffine

Finally the class `WeierstrassProjective`, which does the projective coordinates specific computations. For the method `toAffineCoordinates` the input is the point in projective coordinates and the output is point in affine coordinates.

```
1  /*
2   * Based on Prime Numbers (Crandall/Pomerance) page 327
3   */
4  public class WeierstrassProjective extends Weierstrass {
5    public Point duplicate(Point p) {..
6    public Point add(Point p1, Point p2) {..
7    public Point toAffineCoordinates(Point p) {..
8  }
```

Listing 2.6: Class WeierstrassProjective

This is the complete architecture for doing computation on elliptic curves, with the restriction, that the elliptic curve has two parameters. The three Weierstraß classes made the arithmetic system Weierstraß-specific. If we implement other elliptic curves with two parameters, then we have an arithmetic system with other elliptic curve speciality.

To visualize the dependencies, we illustrate the arithmetic system for elliptic curves with a class diagram[13] in Figure 2.12.

2.5.2. Algorithmic perspective

After showing the architecture of the *elliptic curve arithmetic system*, we will focus in this section on the algorithmic view. Basically this is the implementation of the group law or a modified form of the group law. The content of this section is based on [10] and [13].

The class `Weierstrass` contains some basic methods for Weierstraß curves[14]. The method `getIdentity()` returns the identity element of the Weierstraß curve.

```
1    public Point getIdentity() {
2      return IDENTITY;
3    }
```

Listing 2.7: Method getIdentity

---

[13]There are some additional methods and variables in the diagram, which are useful for the computations. But for the explanation of the relationships they are not relevant.
[14]No matter if either projective or affine coordinates.

The value of IDENTITY is shown in Listing 2.4.

For all computations we need a modulo reduction functionality. This will be done by the class FiniteOperator. The variable name used in the consuming classes for FiniteOperator will be fo.

```
1  public class FiniteOperator {
2    private BigInteger n;
3    public void init(BigInteger n) {
4      this.n = n;
5    }
6    public BigInteger add(BigInteger a, BigInteger b) {
7      return a.add(b).mod(n);
8    }
9    public BigInteger multiply(BigInteger a, BigInteger b) {
10     return a.multiply(b).mod(n);
11   }
12   public BigInteger subtract(BigInteger a, BigInteger b) {
13     return a.subtract(b).mod(n);
14   }
15   public BigInteger negate(BigInteger a) {
16     return a.negate().mod(n);
17   }
18   public BigInteger divide(BigInteger a, BigInteger b) {
19     return a.multiply(b.modInverse(n)).mod(n);
20   }
21   public BigInteger pow(BigInteger a, BigInteger exponent) {
22     return a.modPow(exponent, n);
23   }
24 }
```

Listing 2.8: Class FiniteOperator

The methods discriminant and jInvariant are straightforward like described in Section 2.1.1.

```
1  public BigInteger discriminant() {
2    // d = 4*a^3+27b^2
3    BigInteger A = fo.multiply(Const.FOUR, fo.pow(a, Const.THREE));
4    BigInteger B = fo.multiply(Const.TWENTYSEVEN, fo.pow(b, Const.TWO));
5    BigInteger C = fo.add(A, B);
6    return C;
7  }
```

Listing 2.9: Method discriminant

```
1  public BigInteger jInvariant() {
2    // j = 1728*(4*a^3)/(4*a^3+27*b^3)
3    BigInteger N1 = fo.multiply(Const.FOUR, fo.pow(a, Const.THREE));
4    BigInteger D2 = fo.multiply(Const.TWENTYSEVEN, fo.pow(b, Const.TWO));
5    BigInteger D1 = fo.add(N1, D2);
6    BigInteger R = fo.divide(N1, D1);
7    BigInteger J = fo.multiply(BigInteger.valueOf(1728), R);
8    return J;
```

```
9     }
```

Listing 2.10: Method jInvariant

The method `isNonSingular` checks if a given curve is non-singular. If the curve is non-singular, then it return the value **true**, otherwise **false**. As mentioned in Section 2.1.2 a curve is non-singular, if the discriminant $\Delta \neq 0$ and this is shown in Listing 2.11.

```
1    public boolean isNonSingular() {
2      boolean ret = true;
3      if (discriminant().equals(Const.ZERO)) {
4        ret = false;
5      }
6      return ret;
7    }
```

Listing 2.11: Method isNonSingular

Let $P_1 = (x, y, 1)$ and $P_2 = (x, -y, 1)$ be two points on an elliptic curve E. If we add them with the group law algorithm defined in Section 2.2.2, we get $P_1 + P_2 = (0, 1, 0) = O$. Hence, the negation is just to reverse the algebraic sign of the coordinate y. This is what the method `negate` exactly implements.

```
1    public Point negate(Point p) {
2      return new Point(p.getX(), fo.negate(p.getY()), p.getZ());
3    }
```

Listing 2.12: Method negate

By using the methods `negate` and `add` it is easy to implement the method `subtract`.

```
1    public Point subtract(Point p1, Point p2) {
2      return add(p1, negate(p2));
3    }
```

Listing 2.13: Method subtract

The methods `toAffineCoordinates`, `duplicate` and `add` differ according to whether we are using the affine or the projective extension of the `Weierstrass` class. Next we describe both extension, `WeierstrassAffine` and `WeierstrassProjective`.

2.5.2.1. Affine version

Doubling a point is implemented by adding the point P to itself.

```
1    public Point duplicate(Point p) {
2      return add(p, p);
3    }
```

Listing 2.14: Method duplicate in class WeierstrassAffine

The method `add` for affine coordiantes is the implementation of the group law algorithm from Section 2.2.2.

```
1    public Point add(Point p1, Point p2) {
2      p1 = modulo(p1, n);
3      p2 = modulo(p2, n);
4      if (p1.getZ().equals(Const.ZERO)) {
5        Point p3 = new Point(p2.getX(), p2.getY(), p2.getZ());
6        return p3;
7      }
8      if (p2.getZ().equals(Const.ZERO)) {
9        Point p3 = new Point(p1.getX(), p1.getY(), p1.getZ());
10       return p3;
11     }
12     BigInteger m = null;
13     if (p1.getX().equals(p2.getX())) {
14       if ( fo.add(p1.getY(), p2.getY()).equals(Const.ZERO)) {
15         return getIdentity();
16       }
17       // m=(3*x1^2+a)/(2*y1)
18       m = fo.divide(fo.add(fo.multiply(Const.THREE,
19                     fo.pow(p1.getX(), Const.TWO)), a),
20                     fo.multiply(Const.TWO, p1.getY()));
21     } else {
22       // m=(y2-y1)/(x2-x1)
23       m = fo.divide(fo.subtract(p2.getY(), p1.getY()),
24                     fo.subtract(p2.getX(), p1.getX()));
25     }
26     // x3=m^2-x1-x2
27     BigInteger x3 = fo.subtract(fo.subtract( fo.pow(m,
28                     Const.TWO), p1.getX()), p2.getX());
29     // y3=m*(x1-x3)-y1
30     BigInteger y3 = fo.subtract(fo.multiply(m,
31                       fo.subtract(p1.getX(), x3)),
32                       p1.getY());
33     Point p3 = new Point (x3, y3, BigInteger.ONE);
34     return p3;
35   }
```

Listing 2.15: Method add in class WeierstrassAffine

The output of method toAffineCoordinates is the same as the input, since there is nothing to do with the point if we are in affine coordinates.

```
1    public Point toAffineCoordinates(Point p) {
2      return p;
3    }
```

Listing 2.16: Method toAffineCoordinates in class WeierstrassAffine

The affine version, especially the method add is not efficient, at least it needs inversions. A more efficient approach (without inversions) is the projective version[15]. But the affine version

[15]For more information about operation count see [13] page 324-329 or the excellent page http://www.hyperelliptic.org/EFD/index.html (11 November, 2011), Explicit-Formulas Database, created by Daniel J. Bernstein and Tanja Lange

is not useless. It is the reference implementation and we can use it for comparisons and test cases.

2.5.2.2. Projective version

The methods `duplicate` and `add` for the projective version are the implementation of the Algorithm 7.2.3 in [13]. This is a projective version implementation for modified projective coordinates, i.e. Jacobian coordinates. Using the triples (X, Y, Z), where if $Z \neq 0$, this corresponds to the affine point $(\frac{X}{Z^2}, \frac{Y}{Z^3})$ on the curve[16].

```
public Point duplicate(Point p) {
  p = modulo(p, n);
  if (p.getY().compareTo(Const.ZERO) == 0
      || p.getZ().compareTo(Const.ZERO) == 0) {
    return getIdentity();
  }
  // M=3x^2+az^4
  BigInteger M = fo.add(fo.multiply(Const.THREE,
                 fo.pow(p.getX(), Const.TWO)),
                 fo.multiply(a, fo.pow(p.getZ(), Const.FOUR)));
  // Z=2yz
  BigInteger Z = fo.multiply(Const.TWO, fo.multiply(p.getY(), p.getZ()));
  // y^2
  BigInteger y2 = fo.pow(p.getY(), Const.TWO);
  // S=4xy^2
  BigInteger S = fo.multiply(Const.FOUR, fo.multiply(p.getX(),
                 fo.pow(p.getY(), Const.TWO)));
  // X=M^2-2S
  BigInteger X = fo.subtract(fo.pow(M, Const.TWO),
                 fo.multiply(Const.TWO, S));
  // Y=M(S-x)-8y2^4
  BigInteger Y = fo.subtract(fo.multiply(M, fo.subtract(S, X)),
                 fo.multiply(Const.EIGHT, fo.pow(y2, Const.TWO)));
  return new Point(X, Y, Z);
}
```

Listing 2.17: Method add in class WeierstrassProjective

```
public Point add(Point p1, Point p2) {
  p1 = modulo(p1, n);
  p2 = modulo(p2, n);
  if (p1.getZ().compareTo(Const.ZERO) == 0) {
    return p2;
  }
  if (p2.getZ().compareTo(Const.ZERO) == 0) {
    return p1;
  }
  BigInteger U1 = fo.multiply(p2.getX(),
                 fo.pow(p1.getZ(), Const.TWO));
```

---

[16]See [13], page 324

```
12    BigInteger U2 =   fo.multiply(p1.getX(),
13                          fo.pow(p2.getZ(), Const.TWO)));
14    BigInteger S1 =   fo.multiply(p2.getY(),
15                          fo.pow(p1.getZ(), Const.THREE)));
16    BigInteger S2 =   fo.multiply(p1.getY(),
17                          fo.pow(p2.getZ(), Const.THREE)));
18    BigInteger W = fo.subtract(U1, U2);
19    BigInteger R = fo.subtract(S1, S2);
20    if (W.compareTo(Const.ZERO) == 0) {
21      if (R.compareTo(Const.ZERO) == 0) {
22        return duplicate(p1);
23      }
24      return getIdentity();
25    }
26    BigInteger T = fo.add(U1, U2);
27    BigInteger M = fo.add(S1, S2);
28    // x3 = r^2-t*w^2
29    BigInteger x3 = fo.subtract( fo.pow(R, Const.TWO),
30               fo.multiply(T, fo.pow(W, Const.TWO)));
31    // y3 = (r*(t*w^2-2*x3) - m*w^3)/2
32    BigInteger y3 = fo.subtract(
33        fo.multiply(R, fo.subtract(fo.multiply(T,
34        fo.pow(W, Const.TWO)),
35        fo.multiply(Const.TWO, x3))),
36        fo.multiply(M, fo.pow(W, Const.THREE)));
37    if (!y3.testBit(0)) {
38      y3 = fo.divide(y3, Const.TWO);
39    } else {
40      y3 = fo.divide(fo.add(n, y3), Const.TWO);
41    }
42    //z3 = z1*z2*w
43    BigInteger z3 = fo.multiply(fo.multiply(p1.getZ(),
44                p2.getZ()), W);
45    Point p3 = new Point(x3, y3, z3);
46    return p3;
47  }
```

Listing 2.18: Method add in class WeierstrassProjective

For transforming the resulting point from projective coordinates to affine coordinates we need an extra method. This will be done by `toAffineCoordinates`. This transforms the projective coordinates (X, Y, Z) to affine coordiantes $(x, y, z) = (\frac{1}{Z^2}, \frac{1}{Z^3}, 1)$.

```
1   public Point toAffineCoordinates(Point p) {
2     // (1/Z^2, 1/Z^3, 1)
3     if (p.getZ().compareTo(Const.ZERO) == 0) {
4       return p;
5     }
6     BigInteger x = fo.divide(Const.ONE, p.getZ());
7     BigInteger y = fo.pow(x, Const.TWO);
8     BigInteger z = fo.multiply(x, y);
9     BigInteger pX = fo.multiply(p.getX(), y);
10    BigInteger pY = fo.multiply(p.getY(), z);
```

```
11    Point q = new Point(pX, pY, Const.ONE);
12    return q;
13  }
```

Listing 2.19: Method toAffineCoordinates in class WeierstrassProjective

2.5.2.3. Addition-subtraction ladder

The easiest way to multiply a point P on an elliptic curve with an integer k is to add k-times P to itself.

$$kP = \underbrace{P + P + \cdots + P}_{k-times} \tag{2.46}$$

This is not very efficient. A better way is to implement a addition-subtraction ladder. A addition-subtraction ladder is a modified binary ladder. The idea is to use the methods `duplicate`, `add` and `subtract` from any elliptic curve and choose the operation depending on the binary representation of k. Since this algorithm is not depending from a certain type of elliptic curve, the implementation of `multiply` is placed in the class `EllipticCurveBase`. The implementation is based on Algorithm 7.2.4 in [13]. For more information about the ladder see page 328 [13].

```
1   public Point multiply(Point p, BigInteger k) {
2     if (bigIntegerToBinary == null) {
3       // class to give a binary representation of a given integer.
4       bigIntegerToBinary = new BigIntegerToBinary();
5     }
6     if (k.compareTo(Const.ZERO) == 0) {
7       return getIdentity();
8     }
9     Point ret = new Point(p.getX(), p.getY(), p.getZ());
10    List<Integer> hh = bigIntegerToBinary.calc(k.multiply(Const.THREE), 2);
11    List<Integer> kk = bigIntegerToBinary.calc(k, 2);
12    for (int b = hh.size() - 1; b >= 2; b--) {
13      ret = duplicate(ret);
14      Integer hb = hh.get(b - 1);
15      Integer kb = 0;
16      if (b <= kk.size()) {
17        kb = kk.get(b - 1);
18      } else {
19        kb = 0;
20      }
21      if (hb == 1 && kb == 0) {
22        ret = add(ret, p);
23      } else if (hb == 0 && kb == 1) {
24        ret = subtract(ret, p);
25      }
26    }
27    return ret;
```

```
28      }
```

Listing 2.20: Method multiply in abstract class EllipticCurveBase

2.5.3. Utility methods and examples

The *elliptic curve arithmetic system* contains some more methods. We will not describe them in detail, since they are only utility methods. In the following examples we will use them and explain shortly what kind of functionality they have[17].

In the first example, we define a projective and an affine elliptic curve and two points on them. After doing addition on both curves, we transform the result of the projective curve to affine coordinates. This should be equal to the result of the addition on the affine curve.

```
1   @Test
2   public void testNoAssertion1() throws Exception {
3       BigInteger a = BigInteger.valueOf(34918);
4       BigInteger b = BigInteger.valueOf(5668);
5       BigInteger n = BigInteger.valueOf(38431);
6       weierstrassProjective.init(a, b, n);
7       weierstrassProjective.show();
8
9       Point p1 = new Point(194,25290,1);
10      Point p2 = new Point(20699,5720,1);
11
12      Point resultProjective = weierstrassProjective.add(p1, p2);
13      log.info("Projective result: "
14      + p1.toString() + " + " + p2.toString() +
15      " = " + resultProjective.toString());
16
17      weierstrassAffine.init(a, b, n);
18      Point resultAffine = weierstrassAffine.add(p1, p2);
19      log.info("Affine result: "
20      + p1.toString() + " + " + p2.toString() +
21      " = " + resultAffine.toString());
22
23      log.info("Projective to affine transformation: " +
24          weierstrassProjective.toAffineCoordinates
25      (resultAffine).toString());
26  }
```

Listing 2.21: Example for addition and projective to affine transformation

We get the following result:

```
1   y^2 = x^3 + 34918*x + 5668
2   Projective result: (194,25290,1) + (20699,5720,1) = (1790,28640,20505)
3   Affine result: (194,25290,1) + (20699,5720,1) = (36769,34685,1)
4   (36769,34685,1)
```

---

[17]For more details, see source code

34

Listing 2.22: Result for addition and projective to affine transformation

In the next example we generate a random elliptic curve with the utility method `randomCurve` and we generates one random point on that curve with the utility method `randomPoint`. Then we multiply the point with 2321233549. With the utility method `isPointOnTheCurve` we check the result if it is on the random curve.

```
1   @Test
2   public void testNoAssertion2() throws Exception {
3       weierstrassProjective.randomCurve(BigInteger.valueOf(100000));
4       weierstrassProjective.show();
5       Point p = weierstrassProjective.randomPoint();
6       p.show();
7       BigInteger k = new BigInteger("2321233549");
8       Point pRes = weierstrassProjective.multiply(p, k);
9       log.info("P*k=" + p.toString() + " * " + k + " = " + pRes.toString());
10      boolean b = weierstrassProjective.isPointOnTheCurve(pRes);
11      log.info("Is the resulting point on the curve? " + b);
12  }
```

Listing 2.23: Example for addition and projective to affine transformation

We get the following result:

```
1   y^2 = x^3 + 42031*x + 25801
2   (53834,61542,1)
3   P*k=(53834,61542,1) * 2321233549 = (53017,72692,6451)
4   Is the resulting point on the curve? true
```

Listing 2.24: Result for addition and projective to affine transformation

For more information, see the source code, it is rich on test cases. There are also other utility classes, which are self-explanatory in context with the test cases.

2.6. Twisted Edwards curve

Edwards curve is a representation of elliptic curves, discovered by Harold M. Edwards[18] in 2007. Bernstein and Lange pointed out several advantages using Edwards form in comparison to Weierstraß form in its application to cryptography[19]. Starting with Edwards curve, they introduced together with Birkner, Joye and Peters *twisted Edwards curve*, which is a generalized form of the Edwards curve. This section is based on their article, for details see [13].

We will extend the elliptic curve arithmetic system by twisted Edwards curve. Therefore we start defining Edwards curve.

---

[18]See [15].
[19]See [4].

Definition 2.6.1. *Let K be a arbitrary field with $char(K) \neq 2$. Then Edwards curve is defined over K by the equation*

$$E : x^2 + y^2 = 1 + dx^2 y^2 \tag{2.47}$$

where d is some scalar and $d \in K \setminus \{0, 1\}$, that is $d(1 - d) \neq 0$.

The sum of two points (x_1, y_1), (x_2, y_2) on the Edwards curve E is

$$(x_1, y_1) + (x_2, y_2) = (\frac{x_1 y_2 + y_1 x_2}{1 + dx_1 x_2 y_1 y_2}, \frac{y_1 y_2 - x_1 x_2}{1 + dx_1 x_2 y_1 y_2}). \tag{2.48}$$

The point $(0, 1)$ is the neutral element of the addition law. The inverse of a point (x_1, y_1) on E is $(-x_1, y_1)$.

The addition law is strongly unified, i.e. it can also be used to double a point, and if d is a nonsquare in K then it works for all pairs of inputs[20].

The point $(0, -1)$ has order 2 and the points $(1, 0)$ and $(-1, 0)$ have order 4. The existence of points of order 4 restricts the number of elliptic curves in Edwards form over K. To overcome this restriction Bernstein, Lange, et al. propose to embed the set of Edwards curves in a larger set of elliptic curves of a similar shape and introduce twisted Edwards curves.

Definition 2.6.2. *Let K be an arbitrary field with $char(K) \neq 2$. Fix distinct non-zero elements $a, d \in K$. The twisted Edwards curve with coefficients a and d is the curve*

$$E : ax^2 + y^2 = 1 + dx^2 y^2. \tag{2.49}$$

An Edwards curve is a twisted curve with $a = 1$.

The j-invariant of the twisted Edward curve is

$$\frac{16(a^2 + 14ad + d^2)^3}{ad(a - d)^4}. \tag{2.50}$$

The following section describes the algorithms for arithmetic on twisted Edwards curves. The algorithms will be given for affine and projective versions. All the information here is a short form description from [5], Section 6. For details about efficiency of the algorithms see [5], Section 7.

---

[20]See 13, Theorem 3.3

2.6.1. Arithmetic on twisted Edwards curves

Let (x_1, y_1), (x_2, y_2) be points on the twisted Edwards curve $E : ax^2 + y^2 = 1 + dx^2 y^2$. The sum of these points on E is

$$(x_1, y_1) + (x_2, y_2) = \left(\frac{x_1 y_2 + y_1 x_2}{1 + d x_1 x_2 y_1 y_2}, \frac{y_1 y_2 - a x_1 x_2}{1 + d x_1 x_2 y_1 y_2} \right). \tag{2.51}$$

The neutral element is $(0, 1)$, and the negative of (x_1, y_1) is $(-x_1, y_1)$. The addition law is *complete*, i.e. it works for all inputs if a is a square in K and d is non-square in K.

With the strongly unified property for addition law, we can give formulae for doubling:

$$x_3 = \frac{2 x_1 y_1}{1 + d x_1^2 y_1^2}, \tag{2.52}$$

$$y_3 = \frac{y_1^2 + a x_1^2}{1 - d x_1^2 y_1^2}. \tag{2.53}$$

To avoid inversions, it is more efficient to work on projective twisted coordinates.

$$(aX^2 + Y^2)Z^2 = Z^4 + dX^2 Y^2. \tag{2.54}$$

The transformation to affine coordinates for $Z_1 \neq 0$ is given by the affine point $(\frac{X_1}{Z_1}, \frac{Y_1}{Z_1})$ on E.

Addition operation in projective twisted coordinates $(X_3, Y_3, Z_3) = (X_1, Y_1, Z_1) + (X_2, Y_2, Z_2)$ is given by the following formulae:

$$
\begin{aligned}
A &= Z_1 Z_2 \\
B &= A^2 \\
C &= X_1 X_2 \\
D &= Y_1 Y_2 \\
E &= dCD \\
F &= B - E \\
G &= B + E \\
X_3 &= AF((X_1 + Y_1)(X_2 + Y_2) - C - D) & (2.55) \\
Y_3 &= AG(D - aC) & (2.56) \\
Z_3 &= FG & (2.57)
\end{aligned}
$$

Doubling in projective twisted coordinates $(X_3, Y_3, Z_3) = 2(X_1, Y_1, Z_1)$ is given by the following formulae:

$$
\begin{aligned}
B &= (X_1 + Y_1)^2 \\
C &= X_1^2 \\
D &= Y_1^2 \\
E &= aC \\
F &= E + D \\
H &= Z_1^2 \\
J &= F - 2H \\
X_3 &= (B - C - D)J & (2.58) \\
Y_3 &= F(E - D) & (2.59) \\
Z_3 &= FJ & (2.60)
\end{aligned}
$$

More information about the formulae and alternative formulae when a is square in K can be found in [5], Section 6.

Now, we are able to integrate the twisted Edwards arithmetic into our elliptic curve arithmetic system.

2.6.2. Implementing the arithmetic of a twisted Edwards curve over finite fields

Like in the implementation of the Weierstraß curve, we first implement an abstract class TwistedEdward which is an extension of the class EllipticCurveBase. The methods in TwistedEdward are also independent from affine and projective version. The class diagram in Figure 2.13 illustrates the dependencies. Note, that every further curve type is easy to integrate into the elliptic curve arithmetic system. We only need to have some theoretical knowledge about the corresponding curve.

The methods getIdentity, isNonSingular, negate and substract are quite the same like in the Weierstraß case, the difference is the value for IDENTITY.

```
1  /*
2   * a*x^2+y^2=1+b*x^2+y^2
3   * Identity: (0:1:1)
4   */
5  private final Point IDENTITY = new Point(Const.ZERO, Const.ONE, Const.ONE);
```
Listing 2.25: Value for IDENTITY

For jInvariant and discriminant we have the following methods.

```
1  public BigInteger jInvariant() {
2    // j = 16(a^2+14*a*b+b^2)^3/(a*b*(a-b)^4)
3    BigInteger N1 = fo.pow(a, Const.TWO);
4    BigInteger N2 = fo.multiply(fo.multiply(BigInteger.valueOf(14), a), b);
```

38

```
5    BigInteger N3 = fo.pow(b, Const.TWO);
6    BigInteger N4 = fo.pow(fo.add(fo.add(N1, N2), N3), Const.THREE);
7    BigInteger nominator = fo.multiply(Const.SIXTEEN, N4);
8    BigInteger denominator = fo.multiply(fo.multiply(a, b),
9        fo.pow(fo.subtract(a, b), Const.FOUR));
10   BigInteger j = fo.divide(nominator, denominator);
11   return j;
12   }
13
14   public BigInteger discriminant() {
15       // disc = a·d·(a-d)
16   BigInteger d = b;
17   BigInteger disc = fo.multiply(fo.multiply(a,d), fo.subtract(a, d));
18   return disc;
19   }
```

Listing 2.26: Methods jInvariant and discriminant

The extension classes TwistedEdwardAffine and TwistedEdwardProjective of
TwistedEdward contain the methods which depend on the choosen coordinate version.

2.6.2.1. Affine version

For the affine version of twisted Edwards curve we have implemented the formulae 2.52 and
2.51. The resulting methods duplicate and add are given as follows.

```
1    public Point duplicate(Point p) {
2        // x3 = 2·x1·y1/(1 + d·x1^2·y1^2)
3    BigInteger x3 = fo.divide(fo.add(
4            fo.multiply(p.getX(), p.getY()),
5            fo.multiply(p.getY(), p.getX())),
6         fo.add(Const.ONE, fo.multiply(fo.multiply(
7            fo.multiply(fo.multiply(b, p.getX()), p.getX()),
8            p.getY()), p.getY())));
9        // y3 = (y1^2 + a·x1^2)/(1 - d·x1^2·y1^2)
10   BigInteger y3 = fo.divide(fo.subtract(
11           fo.multiply(p.getY(), p.getY()),
12           fo.multiply(fo.multiply(a, p.getX()),p.getX())),
13             fo.subtract(Const.ONE, fo.multiply(fo.multiply(fo.multiply(
14             fo.multiply(b, p.getX()), p.getX()), p.getY()), p.getY())));
15   return new Point(x3, y3, Const.ONE);
16   }
17
18   public Point add(Point p1, Point p2) {
19   p1 = modulo(p1, n);
20   p2 = modulo(p2, n);
21   BigInteger Zx3 = fo.add(fo.multiply(p1.getX(), p2.getY()),
22               fo.multiply(p1.getY(), p2.getX()));
23   BigInteger Nx3 = fo.add(Const.ONE,
24       fo.multiply(fo.multiply(
25       fo.multiply(fo.multiply(b, p1.getX()),
26       p2.getX()), p1.getY()), p2.getY()));
```

```
27      BigInteger Zy3 = fo.subtract(fo.multiply(p1.getY(), p2.getY()),
28          fo.multiply( a, fo.multiply(p1.getX(), p2.getX())) );
29      BigInteger Ny3 = fo.subtract(Const.ONE,
30          fo.multiply(fo.multiply(
31          fo.multiply(b, p1.getX()),
32          p2.getX()), p1.getY()), p2.getY()));
33      // x3 = (x1*y2 + y1*x2)/(1 + d*x1*x2*y1*y2)
34      BigInteger x3 = fo.divide(Zx3, Nx3);
35      // y3 = (y1*y2 + a*x1*x2)/(1 + d*x1*x2*y1*y2)
36      BigInteger y3 = fo.divide(Zy3,Ny3);
37      Point ret = new Point(x3, y3, Const.ONE);
38      return ret;
39  }
```

Listing 2.27: Methods duplicate and add

Like the affine Weierstraß curve the output of method `toAffineCoordinates` is the same as the input, since there is nothing to do with the point if we are in affine coordinates.

2.6.2.2. Projective version

The implementation of the projective version for twisted Edwards curves is also straight forward. We just transform the given formulae into a piece of source code. The methods `duplicate`, `add` and `toAffineCoordinates` are listed as follows.

```
1
2   public Point duplicate(Point p) {
3       BigInteger B = fo.pow(fo.add(p.getX(), p.getY()), Const.TWO);
4       BigInteger C = fo.pow(p.getX(), Const.TWO);
5       BigInteger D = fo.pow(p.getY(), Const.TWO);
6       BigInteger E = fo.multiply(a, C);
7       BigInteger F = fo.add(E, D);
8       BigInteger H = fo.pow(p.getZ(), Const.TWO);
9       BigInteger J = fo.subtract(F, fo.multiply(Const.TWO, H));
10      // X3= (B-C-D)*J
11      BigInteger X3 = B.subtract(C).mod(n).subtract(D).mod(n).
12                  multiply(J).mod(n);
13      // Y3 = F*(E-D)
14      BigInteger Y3 = F.multiply(E.subtract(D).mod(n)).mod(n);
15      // Z3 = F*J
16      BigInteger Z3 = F.multiply(J).mod(n);
17      return new Point(X3, Y3, Z3);
18  }
19
20  public Point add(Point p1, Point p2) {
21      p1 = modulo(p1, n);
22      p2 = modulo(p2, n);
23      BigInteger A = fo.multiply(p1.getZ(), p2.getZ());
24      BigInteger B = fo.pow(A, Const.TWO);
25      BigInteger C = fo.multiply(p1.getX(), p2.getX());
26      BigInteger D = fo.multiply(p1.getY(),p2.getY());
```

40

```
27    BigInteger E = fo.multiply(b, fo.multiply(C, D));
28    BigInteger F = fo.subtract(B, E);
29    BigInteger G = fo.add(B, E);
30    //X3 = A*F*((X1+Y1)*(X2+Y2)-C-D
31    BigInteger X3 = fo.multiply(fo.multiply(A, F),
32        fo.subtract(fo.subtract(fo.multiply(
33        fo.add(p1.getX(), p1.getY()),
34        fo.add(p2.getX(), p2.getY())), C), D));
35    //Y3 = A*G*(D-a*C)
36    BigInteger Y3 = fo.multiply(fo.multiply(A, G),
37                fo.subtract(D, fo.multiply(a, C)));
38    //Z3 = F*G
39    BigInteger Z3= fo.multiply(F, G);
40    return new Point(X3, Y3, Z3);
41    }
42
43  public Point toAffineCoordinates(Point p) {
44    Point pRet = null;
45    BigInteger x = null;
46    BigInteger y = null;
47    if (p.getZ().compareTo(Const.ZERO) == 0) {
48      pRet = getIdentity();
49    } else {
50      x = fo.divide(p.getX(), p.getZ());
51      y = fo.divide(p.getY(), p.getZ());
52      pRet = new Point(x, y, Const.ONE);
53    }
54    return pRet;
55  }
```

Listing 2.28: Methods duplicate and add and toAffineCoordinates

Hence the implementation for twisted Edwards curves is completely explained. There are many test cases in the source code. With them, we can comprehend how the implementation of twisted Edwards curves really works.

2.6.3. Birational transformations between twisted Edwards curve and Weierstraß curve

To set up a connection between twisted Edwards curves and Weierstraß curves, we need a *rule* where we can express the parameters of the one curve with the parameters of the other. To develop this connection we introduce *Montgomery* curves.

Definition 2.6.3. *Let K be a field with $char(K) \neq 3$. Fix $A \in K \setminus \{-2, 2\}$ and $B \in K \setminus \{0\}$. The Montgomery curve with coefficients A and B is the curve*

$$E_{M,A,B} : Bv^2 = u^3 + Au^2 + u. \tag{2.61}$$

Theorem 3.2 in [5] says, that every twisted Edwards curve over K is birationally equivalent over K to a Montgomery curve and converserly, every Montgomery curve over K is birationally equivalent over K to a twisted Edwards curve. The mapping rules are given in the theorem and will be shown and used immediately. After having the Montgomery curve, we will develop a birationally equivalent to the well known Weierstraß curve in short form and vice versa.

To avoid any possibility of confusion, we use different variable and parameter names in the three curve types. In a nutshell

$$
\begin{aligned}
E_{TE,a,d}: \quad ax^2 + y^2 &= 1 + dx^2y^2 \text{ Twisted Edwards curve,} && (2.62) \\
E_{M,A,B}: \quad Bv^2 &= u^3 + Au^2 + u \text{ Montgomery curve,} && (2.63) \\
E_{W,a',b'}: \quad r^2 &= s^3 + a's + b' \text{ Weierstraß curve in short form.} && (2.64)
\end{aligned}
$$

2.6.3.1. From twisted Edwards curve to Weierstraß curve

Transforming $E_{TE,a,d}$ to $E_{M,A,B}$ is given by the maps

$$
\begin{aligned}
A &= \frac{2(a+d)}{a-d}, && (2.65) \\
B &= \frac{4}{a-d}. && (2.66)
\end{aligned}
$$

The proof is given in [5], Section 3.

The implementation of this transformation is given in the following listing.

```
1   /* Based on Theorem 3.2 in article
2    * Twisted Edwards curves by Daniel J. Bernstein et. al.
3    * In AFRICACRYPT 2008, volume 5023 of LNCS,
4    * pages 389-405. Springer, 2008.
5    */
6   public Montgomery twistedEdward2Montgomery(TwistedEdward te) {
7       BigInteger n=te.getN();
8       fo.init(n);
9       Montgomery mont = new MontgomeryAffine();
10      // A = 2*(a+d)/(a-d)
11      BigInteger A = fo.multiply(Const.TWO,
12                  fo.divide(fo.add(te.getA(), te.getB()),
13                  fo.subtract(te.getA(), te.getB()))));
14      // B = 4/(a-d)
15      BigInteger B = fo.divide(Const.FOUR,
16                  fo.subtract(te.getA(), te.getB()));
17      mont.init(A, B, n);
18      return mont;
19  }
```

Listing 2.29: Method twistedEdward2Montgomery

By dividing $Bv^2 = u^3 + Au^2 + u$ by B^3, we get

$$\frac{1}{B^2}v^2 = \frac{1}{B^3}u^3 + \frac{A}{B^3}u^2 + \frac{1}{B^3}u. \tag{2.67}$$

Replace the variable u and v, with $t = \frac{u}{B}$ and $r = \frac{v}{B}$.

$$r^2 = t^3 + \frac{A}{B}t^2 + \frac{1}{B^2}t. \tag{2.68}$$

By replacing t by $s - \frac{A}{3B}$, we get

$$r^2 = \left(s - \frac{A}{3B}\right)^3 + \frac{A}{B}\left(s - \frac{A}{3B}\right)^2 + \frac{1}{B^2}\left(s - \frac{A}{3B}\right), \tag{2.69}$$

$$r^2 = s^3 + \frac{3 - A^2}{3B^2}s + \frac{2A^3 - 9A}{27B^3}. \tag{2.70}$$

Therefore, we have

$$a' = \frac{3 - A^2}{3B^2}, \tag{2.71}$$

$$b' = \frac{2A^3 - 9A}{27B^3}. \tag{2.72}$$

The implementation of this transformation is given in the following listing.

```
1    public Weierstrass montgomery2Weierstrass(Montgomery mont) {
2      Weierstrass w = new WeierstrassAffine();
3      BigInteger n = mont.getN();
4      fo.init(n);
5      // (3-A^2)/(3*B^2)
6      BigInteger a =
7          fo.divide(fo.subtract(Const.THREE,
8                  fo.pow(mont.getA(), Const.TWO)),
9                    fo.multiply(Const.THREE,
10                   fo.pow(mont.getB(), Const.TWO)));
11     // (2*A^3-9*A)/(27*B^3)
12     BigInteger b =
13       fo.divide(fo.subtract(fo.multiply(Const.TWO,
14             fo.pow(mont.getA(), Const.THREE)),
15             fo.multiply(BigInteger.valueOf(9), mont.getA())),
16             fo.multiply(Const.TWENTYSEVEN,
17             fo.pow(mont.getB(), Const.THREE)));
18     w.init(a, b, n);
19     return w;
20   }
```

Listing 2.30: Method montgomery2Weierstrass

The following listing shows the combination of this two methods. Then we get the transformation from twisted Edwards curve $E_{TE,a,d}$ to Weierstrass curve $E_{W,a',b'}$.

```
1    public Weierstrass twistedEdward2Weierstrass(TwistedEdward te) {
2      return montgomery2Weierstrass (twistedEdward2Montgomery(te));
3    }
```

Listing 2.31: Method twistedEdward2Weierstrass

2.6.3.2. From Weierstraß curve to twisted Edwards curve

In [21] Section 4, K. Okeya et al. prove a proposition relative to transformability from the Weierstraß curve to the Montgomery curve.

Proposition 2.6.4. *A Weierstraß curve* $E_{W,a',b'} : r^2 = s^3 + a's + b'$ *is transformable to the Montgomery curve if and only if it satisfies two conditions as follows:*

1. *The equation* $s^3 + a's + b' = 0$ *has at least one root in* $\mathbb{F}_q$.

2. *The number* $3\alpha^2 + a'$ *is a quadratic residue in* $\mathbb{F}_q$, *where* α *is a root of the equation* $s^3 + a's + b' = 0$ *in* $\mathbb{F}_q$.

The proof of this proposition develops the following identities. Let ν be one of the square roots of

$$\frac{1}{3\alpha^2 + a'} \text{ over } \mathbb{F}_q. \tag{2.73}$$

Then we get

$$B = \nu^3, \tag{2.74}$$
$$A = 3\alpha\nu. \tag{2.75}$$

Notice, if the conditions in Proposition 2.6.4 are not valid, then there exists no Montgomery form. Notice also, for one Weierstrass curve we can get up to three Montgomery curves. That is why the following method `weierstrass2Montgomery` returns a list of Montgomery curves.

```
1    /* Based on article: Elliptic Curves with Montgomery-Form and Their
2     * Cryptographic Applications. Katsuyuki Okeya et. al.
3     * PKC 2000, LNCS 1751, pp. 238-257, 2000.
4     */
5    public List<Montgomery> weierstrass2Montgomery(Weierstrass w) {
6      BigInteger n=w.getN();
7      fo.init(n);
8      List<Montgomery> montList = new ArrayList<Montgomery>();
9      Context ctx = new Context();
10     BigInteger[] pow1 = { Const.ZERO, Const.ONE, Const.THREE};
11     BigDecimal[] coeff1 = { new BigDecimal(w.getB()),
```

```
12                        new BigDecimal(w.getA()),
13                        BigDecimal.ONE};
14      Polynomial polynomial = Polynomial.
15                        polynomialFactory(pow1, coeff1, ctx);
16      List<Complex> roots = polynomial.modRoots(n);
17      // The equation s^3+as+b=0 has at least one root in Fq
18      for (Complex root : roots) {
19        BigInteger alpha = root.getRe().toBigInteger();
20        BigInteger nu2 = Const.THREE.multiply(alpha.pow(2)).add(w.getA());
21        // nu = sqrt(1/nu2)
22        BigInteger nu = sqrtModpShanksTonelli.calc(
23                        fo.divide(Const.ONE, nu2), n);
24        if (nu != null) {
25          BigInteger A = Const.THREE.multiply(alpha).multiply(nu);
26          if (A != null) {
27            BigInteger B = fo.pow(nu, Const.THREE);
28            Montgomery mont = new MontgomeryAffine();
29            mont.init(A, B, n);
30            montList.add(mont);
31          }
32        }
33      }
34      if (montList.size() == 0) {
35        throw new RuntimeException("No Montgomery curve exists!");
36      }
37      return montList;
38    }
```

Listing 2.32: Method weierstrass2Montgomery

Transforming $E_{M,A,B}$ to $E_{TE,a,d}$ is given by the maps

$$a = \frac{A+2}{B}, \tag{2.76}$$
$$d = \frac{A-2}{B}. \tag{2.77}$$

for a fixed A in a field without 2 and -2 and fixed B in a field without 0.

The proof is given in [5], Section 3.

The implementation of this transformation is given in the following listing.

```
1   /* Based on Theorem 3.2 in article
2    * Twisted Edwards curves by Daniel J. Bernstein et. al.
3    * In AFRICACRYPT 2008, volume 5023 of LNCS, pages 389-405. Springer, 2008.
4    */
5   public TwistedEdward montgomery2TwistedEdward(Montgomery mont) {
6     // A=2 or A=-2 or B=0 --> No curve exists
7     if (mont.getA().compareTo(Const.TWO) == 0 ||
8       mont.getA().compareTo(Const.TWO.negate()) == 0 ||
9       mont.getB().compareTo(Const.ZERO) == 0) {
```

```
10      throw new RuntimeException("No twisted Edwards curve exists!");
11    }
12    BigInteger n=mont.getN();
13    fo.init(n);
14    TwistedEdward te = new TwistedEdwardAffine();
15    // a=(A+2)/B
16    BigInteger a = fo.divide( fo.add(mont.getA(),
17                      Const.TWO), mont.getB());
18    // d=(A-2)/B
19    BigInteger d = fo.divide( fo.subtract(mont.getA(),
20                      Const.TWO), mont.getB());
21    te.init(a, d, n);
22    return te;
23  }
```

Listing 2.33: Method montgomery2TwistedEdward

The transformation from Weierstrass curve $E_{W,a',b'}$ to twisted Edwards curve $E_{TE,a,d}$ we get by combining the last two methods.

```
1    public TwistedEdward weierstrass2TwistedEdward(Weierstrass w) {
2      return montgomery2TwistedEdward(weierstrass2Montgomery(w).get(0));
3    }
```

Listing 2.34: Method weierstrass2TwistedEdward

2.6.3.3. Test case

The following test case generates a random Weierstraß curve weierstrass, transforms this to twisted Edwards curve *te* and again back to Weierstraß curve *we*. We expect the *j*-invariant of weierstrass must be equal to *j*-invariant of we.

```
1   @Test
2   public void testWeierstrass2TwistedEdwardAndBack() throws Exception {
3     BigInteger start = new BigInteger("10").pow(25);
4     BigInteger end = new BigInteger("10").pow(20);
5     RandomInteger r = new RandomInteger();
6     BigInteger n = r.nextRandomBigInteger(start, end)
7         .nextProbablePrime();
8
9     Weierstrass weierstrass = new WeierstrassAffine();
10    weierstrass.randomCurve(n);
11    weierstrass.show();
12    log.info(weierstrass.jInvariant());
13    try {
14      TwistedEdward te = curveTransformer.
15                weierstrass2TwistedEdward(weierstrass);
16      te.show();
17      Weierstrass we = curveTransformer.twistedEdward2Weierstrass(te);
18      we.show();
19      log.info("j-invariant weierstrass: " + weierstrass.jInvariant());
20      log.info("j-invariant we: " + we.jInvariant());
```

```
21      Assert.assertTrue(weierstrass.jInvariant().
22                           compareTo(we.jInvariant()) == 0);
23    } catch (RuntimeException e) {
24      log.info(e.getMessage());
25    }
26  }
```

Listing 2.35: Test case testWeierstrass2TwistedEdwardAndBack

Three results of the test case is given as follows.

```
1   TEST 1:
2   y^2 = x^3 + 3140778788765797803*x + 7593447212286110312
3   (3266419971177056115*x^2 + y^2) = 1 + 2649331054599271805*x^2*y^2
4   y^2 = x^3 + 2183161604489028900*x + 3517165223044761536
5   j-invariant weierstrass: 2059866779379991488
6   j-invariant we: 2059866779379991488
7   ------------------------------------------------------------
8   TEST 2:
9   y^2 = x^3 + 1241683878855646046*x + 789459831893036479
10  (649499530684319477*x^2 + y^2) = 1 + 993601907906856890*x^2*y^2
11  y^2 = x^3 + 1241683878855646046*x + 789459831893036479
12  j-invariant weierstrass: 884695979713994238
13  j-invariant we: 884695979713994238
14  ------------------------------------------------------------
15  TEST 3:
16  y^2 = x^3 + 2332687229899967836*x + 7455034418314243941
17  No Montgomery curve exists!
```

Listing 2.36: Three runs of the test case testWeierstrass2TwistedEdwardAndBack

2.7. Conclusion to chapter elliptic curves

This chapter introduced the basics of elliptic curves with respect to theoretical and arithmetical aspects. After showing the existence of a natural group structure on elliptic curves and its group law algorithm, we discussed the algebraic group structure on elliptic curves. With a few example fields, like $\mathbb{R}$, $\mathbb{C}$ and $\mathbb{Q}$ we gave an impression of how the group structure changes according to which field was choosen. In a separate section, we introduced elliptic curves over finite fields and Hasse's theorem, which is the most important theorem with respect to finite fields. The proof of Hasse's theorem outlined further important facts about elliptic curves over finite fields. Especially the estimation of the order of $E(K)$ and the categorizing of the mappings between elliptic curves will become useful in the next chapter.

In addition to the general theoretical subjects, we introduced the arithmetics of two elliptic curves. Weierstraß curve as the reference curve and twisted Edwards curve as an example of a different form of an elliptic curve. Both curves with their arithmetic are implemented into a Java-based elliptic curve arithmetic system. The code developed in this chapter will lay the foundations for the development in the next chapters.

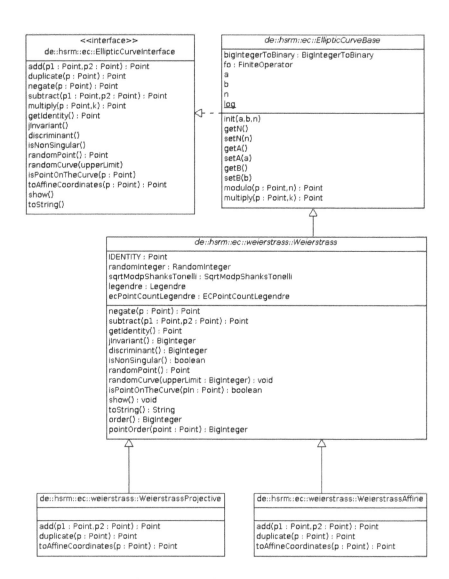

Figure 2.12.: Class diagram of the elliptic curve arithmetic system

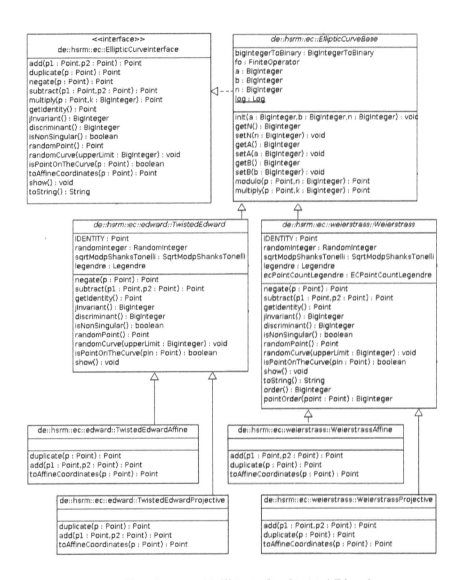

Figure 2.13.: Class diagram with Weierstraß and twisted Edwards curve

Chapter 3.

Construction of elliptic curves with CM

In the last chapter, we discussed the types of elliptic curves and their algebraical and arithmetical properties. In this chapter, we will show how to construct elliptic curves over finite fields $\mathbb{F}_q$. More precisely, we are looking for an approach where we can identify the parameters a, b and q which satisfy the elliptic curve condition together with the order on that determined curve. The elliptic curve type for the development will be the well known Weierstraß form.

The most straightforward approach is given in Listing 3.1. There, we generate the parameters of a possible elliptic curve in Weierstraß form and loop until the elliptic curve condition is satisfied.

```
public void randomCurve(BigInteger upperLimit) {
    BigInteger k = randomInteger.
                    nextRandomBigInteger(Const.THREE, upperLimit);
    BigInteger a = randomInteger.
                    nextRandomBigInteger(Const.ONE, k);
    BigInteger b = randomInteger.
                    nextRandomBigInteger(Const.ONE, k);
    BigInteger q = randomInteger.
                    nextRandomBigInteger(Const.THREE, k).nextProbablePrime();
    init(a, b, q);
    while (!this.isNonSingular()) {
        k = randomInteger.nextRandomBigInteger(Const.ONE, upperLimit);
        a = randomInteger.nextRandomBigInteger(Const.ONE, k);
        b = randomInteger.nextRandomBigInteger(Const.ONE, k);
        q = upperLimit.nextProbablePrime();
        init(a, b, q);
    }
}
```

Listing 3.1: Method randomCurve

By using the Legendre symbol

$$\left(\frac{n}{q}\right) = \begin{cases} -1 & \text{if } n \text{ is a non-square in } \mathbb{F}_q \\ 0 & \text{if } n = 0 \text{ in } \mathbb{F}_q \\ 1 & \text{if } n \text{ is a square in } \mathbb{F}_q, \end{cases} \tag{3.1}$$

50

we can write a formula to count the points on $E(\mathbb{F}_q)$.

$$\#E(\mathbb{F}_q) = q + 1 + \sum_{x \in \mathbb{F}_q} \left(\frac{x^3 + ax + b}{q} \right). \tag{3.2}$$

The implementation of this formula requires furthermore the class `Legendre`[21].

```
1    public BigInteger order(BigInteger a, BigInteger b, BigInteger q) {
2        BigInteger order = q.add(Const.ONE);
3        for (BigInteger x = Const.ZERO;
4                    x.compareTo(q) == -1;
5                    x = x.add(Const.ONE)) {
6            BigInteger y2 = x.pow(3).add(a.multiply(x)).add(b);
7            int res = legendre.symbol(y2, q);
8            order = order.add(BigInteger.valueOf(res));
9        }
10       return order;
11   }
```

Listing 3.2: Method order

The next listing shows, how we use these two implementations in a test case.

```
1    @Test
2    public void testGenerateAndPointCountNoAssertion() throws Exception {
3        BigInteger upperLimit = new BigInteger("100000");
4        weierstrassAffine.randomCurve(upperLimit);
5        weierstrassAffine.show();
6        BigInteger a = weierstrassAffine.getA();
7        BigInteger b = weierstrassAffine.getB();
8        BigInteger q = weierstrassAffine.getN();
9        log.info("q: " + q);
10       BigInteger pointCount = ecPointCountLegendre.order(a, b, q);
11       log.info("order: " + pointCount);
12   }
```

Listing 3.3: Test case for generating and counting the points on an elliptic curve

The result is given in Listing 3.4.

```
1    y^2 = x^3 + 8414*x + 19208
2    q: 22229
3    order: 22210
```

Listing 3.4: Result of the test case

The process of getting an elliptic curve over a finite field with the information about its order is splitted into two steps. We first construct a curve and then count the points on that curve.

Counting points on elliptic curves over finite fields is an active area of research, so that using the Formula 3.2 is indeed the easiest but practically the most inefficient approach. A more

---

[21]See Algorithm 2.3.5 in [5], page 98 and the source code delivered with this thesis.

efficient way for example is the Shanks-Mestre algorithm[22] which is using the *baby-step giant-step*[23] method. Another most celebrated and theoretical sophisticated algorithm is the Schoof's algorithm described in [24]. Rene Schoof's algorithm has a polynomial runtime and is also very interesting regarding to the theory of elliptic curves.

A kind of converse approach to *generating-and-point-counting* method is to determine the curve parameters for a given prime q and a non-negative number N in the Hasse interval $[q + 1 - 2\sqrt{q}, q + 1 + 2\sqrt{q}]$. The prime number q is the order of the prime field $\mathbb{F}_q$ and N is the order of the wanted elliptic curve over $\mathbb{F}_q$. This approach is of great importance in cryptography and can be denoted as *constructing of elliptic curves of prescribed order*. We will shortly discuss this approach in Section 3.11. The discussion will be based on [8]. A complete practical implementation will be not given.

For primality proving, which we will discuss in the next chapter, we can weaken the requirement of *constructing of elliptic curves of prescribed order*. There, we only need a prime number q to construct the elliptic curve. The prime number q is the order of the prime field $\mathbb{F}_q$. This delivers also the parameters of the elliptic curve, but the order N of the elliptic curve is not prescribed. We call this *constructing of elliptic curves for a given prime q*. A complete implementation to this approach will be developed and implemented.

Both of the converse approaches use elliptic curves with *complex multiplication* (CM). In this chapter we will develop the algorithms for curve construction with CM. With support of [4] and [5] we will implement continuously the algorithms into a Java program.

3.1. Hasse's theorem and the trace of Frobenius

In the previous chapter, we proved Hasse's theorem. Remember the insights from the proof with respect to the Frobenius endomorphism.

1. The kernel of $\phi_q - 1$ is equal to $E(\mathbb{F}_q)$.

2. $\phi_q - 1$ is separable, so $\#ker(\phi_q - 1) = deg(\phi_q - 1)$.

3. Proposition 2.4.12 (relationship between degrees and endomorphisms).

For the final proof we defined t with the relation

$$\#E(\mathbb{F}_q) = q + 1 - t. \tag{3.3}$$

The quantity t is called the *trace of Frobenius* at q. The trace of Frobenius t and the Frobenius map ϕ_q are linked by the endomorphism.

$$\phi_q^2 - [t]\phi_q + [q] = [0], \tag{3.4}$$

---

[22]See [5] Algorithm 7.5.3 on, page 350
[23]See [4], Algorithm 5.4.1 on page 241

for a point $P = (x, y)$ on the Weierstraß curve $E(\mathbb{F}_q)$, we have

$$(x^{q^2}, y^{q^2}) - [t](x^q, y^q) + [q](x, y) = O. \tag{3.5}$$

The proof is in [30], page 101/102. Note that $[t]$ and $[q]$ are mappings and not just simple integers. Note also, that $\phi_q^2 - [t]\phi_q + [q]$ is an endomorphism. If we express this endomorphism by an usual quadratic equation, we use the variable π. That is,

$$\pi^2 - t\pi + q = 0 \tag{3.6}$$

is called the *characteristic polynomial* of Frobenius.

With the trace of Frobenius t, we can classify $E(\mathbb{F}_q)$.

Definition 3.1.1. *An elliptic curve E defined over a field $\mathbb{F}_q$ of characteristic p is supersingular if $p \mid t$, where $t = q + 1 - \#E(\mathbb{F}_q)$. If $p \nmid t$ then E is ordinary.*

For a more profound definition of singular/ordinary elliptic curves see [27], page 137. In cryptography, the classifying of $E(\mathbb{F}_q)$ plays an important role. See [6] for more information.

The following proposition enables an easier classification of elliptic curves expressed with trace of Frobenius t.

Proposition 3.1.2. *Let E be an elliptic curve over $\mathbb{F}_q$, where q is a power of the prime number p. Let $t = q + 1 - \#E(\mathbb{F}_q)$. Then E is supersingular if and only if $t \equiv 0 \pmod{p}$, which is if and only if $\#E(\mathbb{F}_q) \equiv 1 \pmod{p}$.*

The proof is in [30], page 130. By implication, an elliptic curve over $\mathbb{F}_q$ is ordinary if $t \not\equiv 0 \pmod{p}$ and for $q = p$, this is just $t \neq 0$.

For curve construction, we are only interested in ordinary curves. If the curve is ordinary, the endomorphism ring of $E(\mathbb{F}_q)$ is isomorphic to an *order in an imaginary quadratic field*, which will be explained soon.

Our aim is to set up all the basics, so that we can connect Hasse's theorem with elliptic curve construction procedure. We begin with the endomorphism ring of an elliptic curve over an arbitrary field K.

3.2. Endomorphism ring of ordinary elliptic curves

In the last chapter, Section 2.4.2, we shortly introduced the endomorphism of an elliptic curve as an isogenie, that is the mapping from an elliptic curve to itself by rational functions. Here, we will study the *structure* of the endomorphism ring of an elliptic curve.

As an example consider an elliptic curve E over an arbitrary field K. If we take a point P from E and add that point to itself, then we get a map

$$[n]\,P \quad : \quad E \to E,$$
$$[n]\,P \quad = \quad \underbrace{P + P + \cdots + P}_{n-times}.$$

Since addition is associative and commutative, it is easy to see that $[n]$ is a homomorphism. Since the mapping is from E to E, $[n]$ is an endomorphism. It is as well easy to show that the set of endomorphisms $End(E(K))$ forms a ring.

What is the structure of $End(E(K))$? $End(E(K))$ contains $[n]$, for every positive integer n. Defining $[-n] : P \to -[n]\,P$, we have that $End(E(K))$ contains $[n]$ for all $n \in \mathbb{Z}$. Thus, for any E, $End(E(K))$ contains $\mathbb{Z}$.

Another interesting example is the Frobenius map for elliptic curves over $\mathbb{F}_q$. The Frobenius map is an endomorphism and satisfies the equation $\pi^2 - t\pi + q = 0$. By solving this quadratic equation for π, we get

$$\pi = \frac{t}{2} \pm \sqrt{\frac{t^2}{4} - q} = \frac{t \pm \sqrt{t^2 - 4q}}{2}.$$

By Hasse's theorem, we have $t^2 - 4q \leq 0$ and write $t^2 - 4q = f^2 D$, for some positive integer f and negative squarefree integer D. The positive integer f is called the *conductor* and the negative squarefree integer D is the *fundamental discriminant*, which will be explained in the following section.

$$\pi = \frac{t \pm f\sqrt{D}}{2}.$$

The solution of the quadratic equation is an element in an imaginary quadratic field $\mathbb{Q}(\sqrt{D})$. Hence, if $t^2 - 4q < 0$ then $End(E(\mathbb{F}_q))$ contains $\mathbb{Z}$ and π, and therefore the ring $\mathbb{Z}[\pi]$.

$$\mathbb{Z}[\pi] \subseteq End(E(\mathbb{F}_q)). \tag{3.7}$$

Three cases can arise, if we completely categorize the structure of an endomorphism ring. Let K be an arbitrary field and E an elliptic curve over K. Then we have

1. $End(E(K)) \cong \mathbb{Z}$.

2. $End(E(K))$ is an order in an imaginary quadratic extension of $\mathbb{Q}$, i.e. $End(E(K)) \cong \mathbb{Z}[\alpha]$ with α imaginary quadratic.

3. $End(E(K))$ is an order in an quaternion algebra.

In the case (1) and (2) the rings are commutative and we have $char(K) = 0$. The ring (3) is not commutative. In cases (2) and (3) the endomorphism ring is over a finite field. The curves in case (2) are ordinary and in case (3) they are supersingular[24].

An abstract proof is given in [27].

For the elliptic curves construction[25] with CM, only the second case is of interest.

3.3. Imaginary quadratic fields and the fundamental discriminant

In this section, we give basic definitions with respect to imaginary quadratic fields. For more details see [23] and [10] (Chapter 5).

Definition 3.3.1. *Imaginary quadratic field.* *A quadratic number field F of the form $\mathbb{Q}(\sqrt{d})$ with $d < 0$, is called an imaginary quadratic field.*

An imaginary quadratic field F is expressed as

$$F = \mathbb{Q}(\sqrt{d}) = \left\{ a + b\sqrt{d} \mid a, b \in \mathbb{Q} \right\}, \tag{3.8}$$

where d is a fixed negative integer.

F is a quadratic field extension of $\mathbb{Q}$, that is, F is a vector space of dimension 2.

Let $\mathcal{O}$ be a ring in F. If every element a of $\mathcal{O}$ is uniquely given by the form $a = \alpha_1 a_1 + \alpha_2 a_2$, where $\alpha_1, \alpha_2 \in \mathbb{Z}$, then $[a_1, a_2]$ is called an *integral basis* of $\mathcal{O}$.

The *maximal order* (largest subring) of F is described by

$$\mathcal{O}_F = [1, \omega] \text{ where } \omega = \begin{cases} \frac{1+\sqrt{d}}{2} \text{ if } d \equiv 1 \pmod 4 \\ \sqrt{d} \text{ if } d \equiv 2, 3 \pmod 4. \end{cases} \tag{3.9}$$

An *order* in an imaginary quadratic field is a ring $\mathcal{O}$ such that

$$\mathbb{Z} \subset \mathcal{O} \subseteq \mathcal{O}_F \text{ and } \mathbb{Z} \neq \mathcal{O}. \tag{3.10}$$

---

[24]See [9].
[25]Note, the constructed curves are in Weierstraß short form.

A fundamental discriminant D is an integer *invariant* in the theory of *integral binary quadratic forms*. The arithmetical aspects of the theory of binary quadratic forms are related to the arithmetic of quadratic fields. It turns out, that there is exactly one quadratic field for every fundamental discriminant $D \neq 1$. If D is negative then there is *exactly one* imaginary quadratic field F for every fundamental discriminant D.

Definition 3.3.2. *Fundamental discriminant*. *An integer D is called a fundamental discriminant if D is the discriminant of a quadratic field F. In other words, $D \neq 1$ and either*

1. *$D \equiv 1 \pmod 4$ and is squarefree or*
2. *$D \equiv 0 \pmod 4$, $\frac{D}{4}$ is squarefree and $\frac{D}{4} \equiv 2, 3 \pmod 4$.*

The maximal order of F expressed with the fundamental discriminant D is described by

$$\mathcal{O}_F = [1, \omega] \text{ where } \omega = \frac{D + \sqrt{D}}{2}. \tag{3.11}$$

In next section, we transform the Definition 3.3.2 into an algorithm.

3.4. Computing the fundamental discriminant

The following listing shows the method `isFundamentalDiscriminant`, which checks if a given negative integer is a fundamental discriminant. This is a implementation of Definition 3.3.2.

```
1   public boolean isFundamentalDiscriminant(BigInteger discriminant) {
2     boolean fundamental = false;
3     // discriminant is not 1
4     boolean A = !(discriminant.compareTo(Const.ONE) == 0);
5     // discriminant = 1 (mod 4)
6     boolean B = discriminant.mod(Const.FOUR).compareTo(Const.ONE) == 0;
7     // discriminant (mod 16) =
8                 ( discriminant (mod 8) or discriminant (mod 12))
9     // this is discriminant/4 = 2,3 (mod 4)
10    boolean C = (discriminant.mod(Const.SIXTEEN).
11                      compareTo(Const.EIGHT) == 0) ||
12               (discriminant.mod(Const.SIXTEEN).
13                      compareTo(Const.TWELVE) == 0);
14    // discriminant/4 is squarefree
15    boolean D = isSquareFree(discriminant.divide(
16                      Const.TWO.pow(integerExponent(discriminant,
17                      Const.TWO).intValue()))));
18    if (A && (B || C) && D) {
19      fundamental = true;
20    }
21    return fundamental;
22  }
```

Listing 3.5: Fundamental discriminant

Here are the first 100 fundamental discriminants computed with this method: -3, -4, -7, -8, -11, -15, -19, -20, -23, -24, -31, -35, -39, -40, -43, -47, -51, -52, -55, -56, -59, -67, -68, -71, -79, -83, -84, -87, -88, -91, -95, -103, -104, -107, -111, -115, -116, -119, -120, -123, -127, -131, -132, -136, -139, -143, -148, -151, -152, -155, -159, -163, -164, -167, -168, -179, -183, -184, -187, -191, -195, -199, -203, -211, -212, -215, -219, -223, -227, -228, -231, -232, -235, -239, -244, -247, -248, -251, -255, -259, -260, -263, -264, -267.

3.5. Ideal and ideal class group

An ideal is a *special* subset of a ring. This section will give a minimum of necessary definitions and facts about ideals so that we can follow the content of this text. For a good and short treatment see [23], pages 85-112.

Definition 3.5.1. *Ideal.* *Let F be a number field and $\mathcal{O}_F$ the maximal order of F. We call a non-empty set $\mathfrak{a} \subset \mathcal{O}_F$ an ideal, if the following conditions for all $a, b \in \mathfrak{a}$ are satisfied:*

1. *If $a, b \in \mathfrak{a}$, then $a + b \in \mathfrak{a}$.*

2. *If $\alpha \in \mathcal{O}_F$ and $a \in \mathfrak{a}$, then $\alpha a \in \mathfrak{a}$.*

If an ideal $\mathfrak{a}$ is generated by an element a of $\mathcal{O}_F$, then $\mathfrak{a} \subset \mathcal{O}_F$ is called the *principal ideal*, in short $\mathfrak{a} = (a)$.

A *proper ideal* of a ring $\mathcal{O}_F$ is strictly smaller than the whole ring. If every single element in a ring $\mathcal{O}_F$ generates a proper ideal, then $\mathcal{O}_F$ is called *principal ideal domain*.

Let $\mathfrak{a}, \mathfrak{b}$ be two non-zero ideals in $\mathcal{O}_F$. If for some $\lambda \in F$ the relation $\mathfrak{a} = \lambda \mathfrak{b}$ holds, then $\mathfrak{a}$ and $\mathfrak{b}$ are equivalent. The ideals, which satisfy $\mathfrak{a} = \lambda \mathfrak{b}$ are equivalent and they form an equivalence class.

It turns out that the ideal classes of $\mathcal{O}_F$ form an abelian group $\mathcal{C}(\mathcal{O}_F)$ called the *ideal class group*. The law of composition is given by $[\mathfrak{a}][\mathfrak{b}] = [\mathfrak{ab}]$. The number of elements in an ideal class group is called the *class number* $h(\mathcal{O}_F) = |\mathcal{C}(\mathcal{O}_F)|$.

3.6. Binary quadratic forms and class number

There is a connection between the theory of binary quadratic forms and the arithmetic of quadratic number fields. For details about binary quadratic forms see [14], pages 128-283.

Definition 3.6.1. *A binary quadratic form f is a function $f(x, y) = ax^2 + bxy + cy^2$ where $a, b, c \in \mathbb{Z}$, denoted in a short form as (a, b, c). We say that f is primitive if $\gcd(a, b, c) = 1$.*

The discriminant of a binary quadratic form is

$$d = b^2 - 4ac. \tag{3.12}$$

If $d < 0$, then the binary quadratic form is called *positiv definite* otherwise *indefinite*. We are only interested in positive definite forms, i.e. we always assume $d < 0$. If the discriminant d of a binary quadratic forms is a fundamental discriminant D, then the form is primitive, i.e $gcd(a,b,c) = 1$. We will only use negative fundamental discriminants for our computations.

A primitive positive definite binary quadratic form relates to an order $\mathcal{O}$ of (fundamental) discriminant D in an imaginary quadratic field F. The following theorem commits this relation.

Theorem 3.6.2. *Let $\mathcal{O}$ be the order of discriminant D in an imaginary quadratic field F.*

1. *If $f(x,y) = ax^2 + bxy + cy^2$ is a primitive positive definite quadratic form of discriminant D, then $[a, \frac{-b+\sqrt{D}}{2}]$ is a proper ideal of $\mathcal{O}$.*

2. *The map sending $f(x,y)$ to $[a, \frac{-b+\sqrt{D}}{2}]$ induces a bijection between the equivalence classes of binary quadratic forms $\mathcal{C}(D)$ and the ideal class group $\mathcal{C}(\mathcal{O})$. Remark, that the class number $h(D) = |\mathcal{C}(D)| = |\mathcal{C}(\mathcal{O})|$.*

For proof, see [18], Theorem 3.1, page 5.

All binary quadratic forms with the same D belong to a same equivalence class. Due to Gauß, it is possible to find a unique *reduced* binary quadratic form in each equivalence class[26].

For any given $D < 0$, the number of the elements in the equivalence class $\mathcal{C}(D)$ is finite and is the *class number* $h(D) = |\mathcal{C}(D)|$.

Knowing $\mathcal{C}(D)$ and $h(D)$ will be useful for the curve construction algorithm, particulary for computing the Hilbert class polynomial.

The algorithm here is based on [20], Section 3.1.3, page 14. The following listing gives a outline of the *data container* for the reduced binary quadratic forms.

```
public class BinaryQuadraticForm implements Serializable {
  private BigInteger a;
  private BigInteger b;
  private BigInteger c;
  public void init(BigInteger a, BigInteger b, BigInteger c) {
    this.a = a;
    this.b = b;
    this.c = c;
  }
  public void init(int a, int b, int c) {
  public void init(BigInteger a,
                   BigInteger b, BigInteger c) { ...
  public BigInteger discriminant() { ...
  public boolean isReduced() { ...
```

[26]See [10], page 232, Lemma 5.3.4.

```
15    public BinaryQuadraticForm reduce() { ...
16    public BigInteger getA() { ...
17    public BigInteger getB() { ...
18    public BigInteger getC() { ...
19    private void euklideanStep() { ...
20 }
```

Listing 3.6: Container for reduced forms

The method `qfList` computes all the reduced binary quadratic forms for a given fundamental discriminant D and adds the result into a list of quadratic forms.

```
1  /*
2   * Based on F.Morain's article
3   * Implementation of the Atkin-Goldwasser-Kilian
4   * Primality Testing Algorithm,
5   * Rapport de Recherche 911, INRIA, Oct. 1989
6   * Section 3.1.3, page 14.
7   */
8  public List<BinaryQuadraticForm> qfList(BigInteger discriminant,
9                                            Context ctx) {
10    List<BinaryQuadraticForm> binaryQuadraticFormList =
11                      new ArrayList<BinaryQuadraticForm>();
12    if (!(discriminant.compareTo(Const.ZERO) == 1)) {
13      BigInteger fundamentalDiscriminant = discriminant.negate();
14      BigInteger r = squareRootBig.sqrtBigInteger(
15            fundamentalDiscriminant.divide(Const.THREE),ctx);
16      BigInteger b = fundamentalDiscriminant.mod(Const.TWO);
17      while (b.compareTo(r) == -1 || b.compareTo(r) == 0) {
18        BigInteger m = b.pow(2).add(fundamentalDiscriminant)
19              .divide(Const.FOUR);
20        BigInteger sm = squareRootBig.sqrtBigInteger(m,ctx);
21        for (BigInteger a = Const.ONE; a.compareTo(sm) == -1
22            || a.compareTo(sm) == 0; a = a.add(Const.ONE)) {
23          if (m.mod(a).compareTo(Const.ZERO) == 0) {
24            BigInteger c = m.divide(a);
25            if (b.compareTo(a) == -1 || b.compareTo(a) == 0) {
26              if (b.compareTo(a) == 0 || c.compareTo(a) == 0) {
27                BinaryQuadraticForm bgf = new BinaryQuadraticForm();
28                bgf.init(a, b, c);
29                binaryQuadraticFormList.add(bgf);
30              } else {
31                BinaryQuadraticForm bgf = new BinaryQuadraticForm();
32                bgf.init(a, b, c);
33                binaryQuadraticFormList.add(bgf);
34                if (!(b.compareTo(Const.ZERO) == 0)) {
35                  bgf = new BinaryQuadraticForm();
36                  bgf.init(a, b.negate(), c);
37                  binaryQuadraticFormList.add(bgf);
38                }
39              }
40            }
41          }
```

```
42        }
43          b = b.add(Const.TWO);
44        }
45    } else {
46        log.info("Only negative discriminant are allowed!");
47    }
48    return binaryQuadraticFormList;
49 }
```

Listing 3.7: List of reduced forms for a valid D

The following test case computes the reduced forms for the discriminant $D = -23$.

```
1    public void test1() throws Exception {
2        Context ctx = new Context(100);
3        BigInteger D = BigInteger.valueOf(-23);
4        List<BinaryQuadraticForm> list = reducedForms.qfList(D,ctx);
5        for (BinaryQuadraticForm binaryQuadraticForm : list) {
6            binaryQuadraticForm.show();
7        }
8    }
```

Listing 3.8: Test case for computing the reduced forms

As a result, we get three elements. Therefore the class number is $h(-23) = 3$.

```
1    D :-23
2    (1, 1, 6)
3    (2, 1, 3)
4    (2, -1, 3)
```

Listing 3.9: Test result for computing the reduced forms

Another interesting test case computes the class numbers for a list of given fundamental discriminants.

```
1    public void test2() throws Exception {
2        Context ctx = new Context(100);
3        List<BigInteger> listFd = fundamentalDiscriminant.fundamentalDiscriminants(
4            BigInteger.valueOf(-5000), BigInteger.valueOf(-4950));
5        for (BigInteger D : listFd) {
6            int classNumber = reducedForms.formClassNumber(D,ctx);
7            log.info("D:" + D + "   " + "classNumber:" + classNumber);
8        }
9    }
```

Listing 3.10: Test case for computing the class numbers for certain fundamental discriminants

First, we generate a list of fundamental discriminants D in a given interval of $[-5000, -4950]$. Then, for each element from the list, we compute the class number.

```
1   D:-4951   classNumber:31
2   D:-4952   classNumber:42
3   D:-4955   classNumber:28
4   D:-4963   classNumber:12
5   D:-4964   classNumber:32
6   D:-4967   classNumber:59
7   D:-4971   classNumber:16
8   D:-4979   classNumber:30
9   D:-4980   classNumber:32
10  D:-4983   classNumber:52
11  D:-4984   classNumber:16
12  D:-4987   classNumber:9
13  D:-4991   classNumber:92
14  D:-4996   classNumber:32
15  D:-4999   classNumber:33
```

Listing 3.11: Test result for computing the class numbers for certain fundamental discriminants

This little example shows, that the class number seems to appear quite randomly. For the curve construction algorithm, we will compute the class numbers for fundamental discriminants in a bigger interval. Then, we will sort the result list ascending first by the class number and second by the fundamental discriminant. In this example, this would be as follows:

```
1   D:-4987   classNumber:9
2   D:-4963   classNumber:12
3   D:-4971   classNumber:16
4   D:-4984   classNumber:16
5   D:-4955   classNumber:28
6   D:-4979   classNumber:30
7   D:-4951   classNumber:31
8   D:-4964   classNumber:32
9   D:-4980   classNumber:32
10  D:-4996   classNumber:32
11  D:-4999   classNumber:33
12  D:-4952   classNumber:42
13  D:-4983   classNumber:52
14  D:-4967   classNumber:59
15  D:-4991   classNumber:92
```

Listing 3.12: Sorting first ascending by class number second by fundamental discriminant

3.7. Modified Cornacchia algorithm

In section 3.2 we received the equation

$$t^2 - 4q = f^2 D \tag{3.13}$$

as a direct consequence of Hasse's theorem.

61

With a little conversion, we get[27]

$$4q = t^2 - f^2 D. \tag{3.14}$$

If we can find a valid t and f for a given q and fundamental discriminant D, then we are able to compute the cardinality of a possible elliptic curve with $\#E(\mathbb{F}_q) = q + 1 - t$.

We will implement an algorithm called the *modified Cornacchia algorithm*. With modified Cornacchia algorithm we are able to solve the equation $4q = t^2 - f^2 D$ for a given q and fundamental discriminant D.

The algorithm of Cornacchia outputs either an integer solution (x, y) to the Diophantine equation $q = x^2 + Ny^2$ for $0 < N$, or outputs that such a solution does not exist[28]. An extended version of this algorithm[29], the modified Cornacchia algorithm, does the same for the equation $4q = x^2 + |N| y^2$. This is exactly what we are looking for, to solve $4q = t^2 - f^2 D$.

The implementation is given in the following listing.

```
1    // Modified Cornacchia algorithm. Implementation is based on
2    // Henri Cohen's book : A course in computational algebraic number theory.
3    // Page 36, Algorithm 1.5.3
4    public ModifiedCornacchiaResult calc(BigInteger p,
5                                         BigInteger d, Context ctx) {
6      ModifiedCornacchiaResult mcr = new ModifiedCornacchiaResult();
7      // initialize the result container
8      mcr.setX(null);
9      mcr.setY(null);
10     // Step 1 [Case p=2]
11     if (p.compareTo(Const.TWO) == 0) {
12       if ( d.add(Const.EIGHT).compareTo(
13           squareRootBig.sqrtBigInteger(
14               d.add(Const.EIGHT), ctx).pow(2)) == 0) {
15         mcr.setX(squareRootBig.sqrtBigInteger(d.add
16                         (Const.EIGHT),ctx));
17         mcr.setY(Const.ONE);
18         return mcr;
19       } else {
20         return mcr;
21       }
22     }
23     // Step 2 [Test if residue]
24     if (legendre.symbol(d, p) == -1) {
25       return mcr;
26     }
27     // Step 3 [Compute square root with modulo with
28     //          Shank-Tonnelli algorithm]
29     BigInteger x0 = sqrtModpShanksTonelli.calc(d, p);
```

---

[27]See Juliana V. Beldings article [2] for an excellent overview about this equation and [12] for more details.
[28]See [10], page 34, Algorithm 1.5.2
[29]See [10], page 36, Algorithm 1.5.3

```
30    if (!(x0.pow(2).mod(Const.TWO).compareTo(d.mod(Const.TWO)) == 0)) {
31      x0 = p.subtract(x0);
32    }
33    // Step 4 [Euclidean algorithm]
34    BigInteger a = Const.TWO.multiply(p);
35    BigInteger b = x0;
36    BigInteger c = squareRootBig.sqrtBigInteger(p,ctx);
37    c = Const.TWO.multiply(c);
38    while (b.compareTo(c) == 1) {
39      BigInteger r = a;
40      a = b;
41      b = r.mod(b);
42    }
43    BigInteger t = Const.FOUR.multiply(p).subtract(b.pow(2));
44    // Step 5 [Test solution]
45    if (!( t.mod(d.abs()).compareTo(Const.ZERO) == 0)) {
46      mcr.setX(null);
47      mcr.setY(null);
48      return mcr;
49    } else {
50      if (!(t.divide(d).negate().compareTo(squareRootBig.
51              sqrtBigInteger(t.divide(d).
52                        negate(),ctx).pow(2)) == 0 )) {
53        mcr.setX(null);
54        mcr.setY(null);
55        return mcr;
56      } else {
57        mcr.setX(b);
58        mcr.setY(squareRootBig.sqrtBigInteger(
59                            t.divide(d.abs()), ctx));
60        return mcr;
61      }
62    }
63  }
```

Listing 3.13: Implemetation of the modified Cornacchia algorithm

The result ModifiedCornacchiaResult is a simple *data container*.

```
1  public class ModifiedCornacchiaResult {
2    private final static Log log = LogFactory.
3                        getLog(ModifiedCornacchiaResult.class);
4    private BigInteger x;
5    private BigInteger y;
6    public BigInteger getX() {
7      return x;
8    }
9    public void setX(BigInteger x) {
10     this.x = x;
11   }
12   public BigInteger getY() {
13     return y;
14   }
```

```
15    public void setY(BigInteger y) {
16      this.y = y;
17    }
18    public void show() {
19      log.info("{" + x + ", " + y + "}");
20    }
21  }
```

Listing 3.14: Result container for Cornacchia algorithm

We describe a possible test case. For p we set the Mersenne prime number $2^{521} - 1$, which has 157 digits. Then we generate a list of fundamental discrimants between -100 and -50. For all this fundamental discriminant, we compute the values for t and f.

```
1    @Test
2    public void testModifiedCornacchiaNoAssertion() throws Exception {
3      // 2^521-1 (157 Digits Mersenne prime number)
4      BigInteger p = Const.TWO.pow(521).subtract(Const.ONE);
5      List<BigInteger> fdList = fundamentalDiscriminant.
6        fundamentalDiscriminants(BigInteger.valueOf(-100),
7                                 BigInteger.valueOf(-50));
8      for (BigInteger d : fdList) {
9        log.info("d: " + d);
10       ModifiedCornacchiaResult mcr = new ModifiedCornacchiaResult();
11       Context ctx = new Context(300);
12       mcr = modifiedCornacchia.calc(p, d, ctx);
13       mcr.show();
14     }
15   }
```

Listing 3.15: Test case modified Cornacchia algorithm

The output of this test case is as follows.

```
1    d: -51
2    {4991357334870116633617473463283965010
3        04749833723524016342302774479852437218705 2,
4      22341127976160940113028892046620875 2
5        29940423114667341987268215135956685439823 0}
6    d: -52
7    {null, null}
8    d: -55
9    {null, null}
10   d: -56
11   {null, null}
12   d: -59
13   {null, null}
14   d: -67
15   {4476462796127788463949927205308716120
16       54882291746926579225330709215239641115577 77,
17     33279619229053375682219837382732441 3
18       20126525586936097498888017185278052245612 5}
19   d: -68
20   {null, null}
```

```
21  d: -71
22  {null, null}
23  d: -79
24  {null, null}
25  d: -83
26  {null, null}
27  d: -84
28  {null, null}
29  d: -87
30  {522894052877864713825278786549241269
31        326432836769956697408019254865134038391 0648,
32      367300789729930939118238265276253417
33      5450877032606393834901069159736434980 6490}
34  d: -88
35  {223081065979035588765565230568250980
36        437662071079814311973699510046418529929 8806,
37      505455177860511951847402040901047439
38      4957349510273516060408778660390865451 86069}
39  d: -91
40  {null, null}
41  d: -95
42  {517129366320438669937008443267768070
43        380114100162733132086526415893065732584 9968,
44      868702898412396775385560797548813528
45      6653031621398834926416503345736274717 2958}
```

Listing 3.16: Output of modified Cornacchia algorithm test case

There are only results for discriminants $-67, -87, -88, -91$ and -95. Let us consider the result for discriminant -95. We know the value of trace Frobenius

$t = 5171293663204386699370084432677680703801141001627331320865264158930657325849996$
8

and the value for the Mersenne prime

$q = 68647976601306097149819007990813932172694353001433054093944634591855431833976560521225596406614545549779631139148085803712198799971664381257402829111505 7151.$

With this, we are able to identify the order of the elliptic curve E defined over $\mathbb{F}_{2^{521}-1}$ with

$\#E(\mathbb{F}_q) = q + 1 - t = 68647976601306097149819007990813932172694353001433054093944634591855431833976508808288964362747551848928636337107770568961203606683957785484150976337892 07184.$

The order of the elliptic curve $E(\mathbb{F}_{2^{521}-1})$ is identified, but the parameters a, b of the elliptic curve are not known. Notice, we decided to use $\#E(\mathbb{F}_q) = q + 1 - t$, i.e. there is another order if we use $\#E(\mathbb{F}_q) = q + 1 + t$ which leads to the order of the quadratic twist of E.

3.8. Construction of elliptic curves with CM

In this section, we want to explain how to produce an elliptic curve with CM[30].

Definition 3.8.1. *CM. If the endomorphism ring $End(E)$ is an order $\mathcal{O}$ of the discriminant d in an imaginary quadratic field $F = \mathbb{Q}(\sqrt{d})$, then we say E has CM.*

The theory of CM is vast and advanced mathematics. This section is mainly oriented on [10],[13] and [1]. For more details see [12],[28],[22] and [25].

The characteristic polynomial 3.6 of Frobenius endomorphism of an elliptic curve E is a quadratic formula. The roots of this quadratic formula lie in an imaginary quadratic field $F = \mathbb{Q}(\sqrt{D})$, where D is the fundamental discriminant. If E is not supersingular, then the endomorphism ring of E is an order in F. Since D is the fundamental discriminant, the order in F is the maximal order $\mathcal{O}_F$.

Let E be an elliptic curve over $\mathbb{C}$. Then E has the form $\mathbb{C}/L$ where L is a lattice[31]. Let $E_1 = \mathbb{C}/L_1$ and $E_2 = \mathbb{C}/L_2$ be two elliptic curves over $\mathbb{C}$. Then E_1 is isomorphic to E_2 if and only if $L_1 = \alpha L_2$ for a certain non-zero $\alpha \in \mathbb{C}$.

The set of mappings from E_1 to E_2 can be identified with the set of $\alpha \in \mathbb{C}$ such that $\alpha L_1 \subset L_2$. That is, the set of endomorphisms of E denoted $End(E)$ is an abelian ring and $End(E)$ is isomorphic to the set of α such that $\alpha L \subset L$.

In Section 2.1.1 we mentioned, that elliptic curves over an arbitrary field $\bar{K}$ are isomorphic if and only if they have the same j-invariant $j(E) = 1728\frac{4a^3}{4a^3+27b^2}$. That is, the function $j(E)$ characterizes the isomorphism class of E over $\bar{K}$.

We will express the function $j(E)$ for E over $\mathbb{C}$. Let $E = \mathbb{C}/L$ be an elliptic curve over $\mathbb{C}$. L can be generated by $\omega_1, \omega_2 \in \mathbb{C}$ where ω_1, ω_2 are linearly independent over $\mathbb{R}$. By multiplying L with $\frac{1}{\omega_1}$ we get $L_\tau = [1, \tau]$, where $\tau = \frac{\omega_2}{\omega_1}$. Since multiplying a lattice by a non-zero complex number does not change the isomorphism class of E, we have $j(E) = j(E_\tau)$. Notice $\tau = \frac{\omega_2}{\omega_1}$ is an element from the upper half of the complex plane, i.e. $\mathbb{H} = \{\tau \in \mathbb{C} \,|\, Im(\tau) > 0\}$. To express this we write

$$j : \mathbb{H} \;\; \rightarrow \;\; \mathbb{C},$$
$$j(\tau) \;\; = \;\; j(E_\tau).$$

If E has CM then the lattice L (as described above) of E is a proper ideal of $\mathcal{O}_F$. We denote this proper ideal with $\mathfrak{a}_L$.

If an elliptic curve E has CM a proper ideal is given by (Theorem 3.6.2(1))

$$\mathfrak{a}_L = \left[a, \frac{-b + \sqrt{D}}{2} \right] \text{ with } a, b \in \mathbb{Z}. \tag{3.15}$$

---

[30]Based on Atkin-Morain approach, for details see [1].
[31]See Section 2.3.2

Remark: a and b are the coefficients of a binary quadratic form. With the method qfList from Section 3.6 we are able to compute all the reduced binary quadratic forms for a given fundamental discriminant D.

Multiplying $\mathfrak{a}_L$ with $\frac{1}{a}$, we get

$$\mathfrak{a}_{L_\tau} = \left[1, \frac{-b + \sqrt{D}}{2a} \right] \text{ with } a, b \in \mathbb{Z}, \tag{3.16}$$

with

$$\tau = \frac{-b + \sqrt{D}}{2a} \text{ with } a, b \in \mathbb{Z}. \tag{3.17}$$

It turns out, that the j-invariant of elliptic curves with CM by $\mathcal{O}_F$ is only depending from a proper ideal of $\mathcal{O}_F$.

$$j(\tau) = j(\mathfrak{a}_{L_\tau}) = j(E_\tau). \tag{3.18}$$

There are $h(\mathcal{O}_F) = h(D)$ different elliptic curves with CM by $\mathcal{O}_F$.

For the maximal order $\mathcal{O}_F$ in F

$$H = F(j(\tau)) \tag{3.19}$$

is an extension of F of degree $h(D)$.

This is in fact the content of the first main theorem of CM:

Theorem 3.8.2. *First main theorem of CM.**Let F be an imaginary quadratic field with maximal order $\mathcal{O}_F$, and let $E(\mathbb{C})$ be an elliptic curve with $End(E) \cong \mathcal{O}_F$. Then $F(j(E))$ is the Hilbert class field H of F.*

The Hilbert class field H is the maximal unramified abelian extension of F. In H every ideal in $\mathcal{O}_F$ becomes principal when considered as an ideal in $\mathcal{O}_H$.

The common minimal polynomial $H_D(x)$ for the j values of the Hilbert class field is characteristic and is called the *Hilbert class polynomial* for $\mathcal{O}_F$. The Hilbert class polynomial for discriminant D is

$$H_D(x) = \prod_{i=1}^{h(D)} \left(x - j\left(\frac{-b_i + \sqrt{D}}{2a_i} \right) \right). \tag{3.20}$$

The coefficients of $H_D(x)$ are integers, since $\mathcal{O}_F$ is a maximal order.

The roots of the Hilbert class polynomial will be used to compute the j values. For the curve construction, we have $F = \mathbb{F}_q = \mathbb{F}_{p^m}$ with p prime. Due to a theorem of Max Deuring

$End(E(\mathbb{F}_q))$ remains the same for *almost all* $E(\mathbb{F}_q)$ if we reduce an elliptic curve with CM over $\mathbb{C}$ by p. That is, we get the j values by computing the roots of $H_D(x)$ in $\mathbb{F}_q$.

Finding the Hilbert class polynomial $H_D(x)$ is necessary for constructing elliptic curves over finite fields with a desired endomorphism ring. In next section, we implement an algorithm for identifiying the Hilbert class polynomial $H_D(x)$.

By plug in one j-value into the Equation 2.8 we get the required parameters of the elliptic curve E. In case of fundamental discriminant $D < -4$ there exist only one twisted curve to E and this can be identifyied by Theorem 2.1.2.

We summarize the steps for generating a elliptic curve with CM-method:

1. For a given prime q and (smallest) $D < -4$ find a t.

2. Compute the orders of E $\#E(\mathbb{F}_q) = q + 1 \pm t$.

3. Compute the Hilbert class polynomial $H_D(x)$.

4. Find a root j_0 of $H_D(x)$ (mod q). j_0 is the j-invariant of the E to be constructed.

5. Set $c = \frac{j_0}{1728 - j_0}$ (mod q) and the elliptic curve will be $E : y^2 = x^3 + 3cx + 2c$.

6. Compute the twist of E using randomly selected quadratic non-residue $g \in \mathbb{F}_q$.

In next section, we will implement an algorithm for computing the Hilbert class polynomial.

3.9. Computing the Hilbert class polynomial

There are a few different methods for computing $H_D(x)$, for example the classical complex analytical method, the p-adic method or the method which uses the chinese remainder theorem.

In this section we will implement and discuss the classical complex analytical method based on [10], pages 414-416. For the other methods, see [3] and [29].

3.9.1. Classes `Complex` and `Polynomial`

In computation of $H_D(x)$ with complex analytical method, the integer coefficients of $H_D(x)$ have complex values during the loop process in the algorithm. Therefore the target data structure `Polynomial` which finally represents $H_D(x)$ has complex coefficients. The coefficients are implemented by the class `Complex`.

The following listing illustrates an outline of class `Complex`, whereby the class by its method names is self-explanatory.

```
1   public class Complex {
2     // Defines the precision of re and im
3     private Context ctx;
4
5     private BigDecimal re;
6     private BigDecimal im;
7
8     public BigDecimal getRe() {
9       return re;
10    }
11    public void setRe(BigDecimal re) {
12      this.re = re;
13    }
14    public BigDecimal getIm() {
15      return im;
16    }
17    public void setIm(BigDecimal im) {
18      this.im = im;
19    }
20    // Constructor methods
21    public Complex() {}
22    public Complex(Context ctx) {...
23    public Complex(BigDecimal re, BigDecimal im, Context ctx) {...
24    public Complex(Double re, Double im, Context ctx) {...
25    // Arithmetical methods
26    public Complex add(Complex z) {...
27    public Complex subtract(Complex z) {...
28    public Complex pow(BigInteger n) {...
29    public Complex multiply(Complex z) {...
30    public Complex square() {...
31    public BigDecimal abs() {...
32    public Complex divide(Complex z) {...
33    public boolean equals(Complex c) {...
34    public boolean isZero() {...
35    public boolean isOne() {...
36    public Complex negate() {...
37    public void show() {...
38  }
```

Listing 3.17: Complex class representing the coefficients of the polynomial

The `Polynomial` class is the most useful utility class of this thesis. The modulo arithmetic methods are mainly based on [10].

```
1   public class Polynomial implements Serializable {
2     @Autowired
3     private SqrtModpShanksTonelli sqrtModpShanksTonelli;
4     @Autowired
5     private Legendre legendre;
6     @Autowired
7     private FiniteOperator fo;
8     @Autowired
9     private RandomInteger randomInteger;
```

69

```java
10  @Autowired
11  private BigIntegerToBinary bigIntegerToBinary;
12  private List<PolynomialComponent> component;
13  private Context ctx;
14
15  // Default constructor
16  public Polynomial() {}
17  // Constructor with precision
18  public Polynomial(Context ctx) {...
19
20  public void setCtx(Context ctx) {...
21  //Constructor creates the Polynomial c0 + c1*x + c2*x^2 + c3*x^3 +...
22  public Polynomial(List<PolynomialComponent> c, Context ctx) {...
23
24  public void setComponent(List<PolynomialComponent> c) {...
25  public List<PolynomialComponent> getComponent() {...
26
27  // Arithmetical methods
28  public BigInteger degree() {...
29  public Polynomial modSubtract(Polynomial poly, BigInteger p) {...
30  public Polynomial modMultiply(Polynomial poly, BigInteger p) {...
31  public Polynomial modQuotient(Polynomial poly, BigInteger p) {...
32  public Polynomial modRemainder(Polynomial poly, BigInteger p) {...
33  public Polynomial modGcd(Polynomial g, BigInteger p) {...
34  public Polynomial modReduction(BigInteger p) {...
35  public Polynomial modPow(BigInteger exp, Polynomial divPoly,
36                      BigInteger p) {...
37  public List<Complex> modRoots(BigInteger p) {...
38  private void roots(List<Complex> rootList, Polynomial poly,
39                   BigInteger p) {...
40  private Polynomial monic(BigInteger p) {...
41  private PolynomialQuotientRemainder modQuotientRemainder(
42                   Polynomial poly, BigInteger p) {...
43
44  // Some utility methods
45  public boolean equals(Polynomial p) {
46  public void clean() {
47  public Polynomial getZero() {
48  public Polynomial getOne() {
49  public boolean isZero() {
50  public boolean isOne() {
51  public static Polynomial polynomialFactory(BigInteger[] pow,
52                   Complex[] coeff, Context ctx) {...
53  public static Polynomial polynomialFactory(BigInteger[] pow,
54                   BigDecimal[] coeff, Context ctx) {...
55  public static Polynomial polynomialFactory(Integer[] pow,
56                   Integer[] coeff, Context ctx) {...
57  public static Polynomial polynomialFactory(String[] pow,
58                   String[] coeff, Context ctx) {...
59  private Polynomial copyPolynomial(Polynomial poly) {...
60  public void show() {...
61  private String showComplex(Complex c) {...
```

```
62
63     }
```

Listing 3.18: Polynomial class

The best way to explain `Polynomial` is to illustrate the functionality of some methods in a test case. The following test case is initializing a polynomial with complex coefficients.

```
1    @Test
2    public void testInitialize() throws Exception {
3        Context ctx = new Context();
4        BigInteger[] pow2 = { BigInteger.valueOf(0), BigInteger.valueOf(2),
5                                          BigInteger.valueOf(4) };
6        Complex[] coeff2 = {
7                new Complex(new BigDecimal("0"), new BigDecimal("-3"), ctx),
8                new Complex(new BigDecimal("3.5"), new BigDecimal("-1.5"), ctx),
9                new Complex(new BigDecimal("2.5"), new BigDecimal("0"), ctx)
10               };
11       Polynomial p2 = Polynomial.polynomialFactory(pow2, coeff2, ctx);
12       p2.show();
13   }
```

Listing 3.19: Test case for initializing a polynomial

```
1    (0,-3)x^0 + (3.5,-1.5)x^2 + (2.5,0)x^4
```

Listing 3.20: Output of test case for initializing a polynomial

In the next test case we do modulo multiplication of two polynomials with integer coefficients.

```
1    @Test
2    public void testMultiply() throws Exception {
3        Context ctx = new Context();
4        BigInteger p = new BigInteger("2063");
5        Integer[] pow1 = { 0, 1, 2, 3, 4};
6        Integer[] coeff1 = { -3772, 1127, 10258, 8872, 3892 };
7        Polynomial p1 = Polynomial.polynomialFactory(pow1, coeff1, ctx);
8        p1.show();
9        Integer[] pow2 = { 0, 1, 0, 3 };
10       Integer[] coeff2 = { 3692, 486, 7296, -4666 };
11       Polynomial p2 = Polynomial.polynomialFactory(pow2, coeff2, ctx);
12       p2.show();
13       p1.modMultiply(p2, p).show();
14   }
```

Listing 3.21: Test case for modulo multiplication

```
1    (-3772,0)x^0 + (1127,0)x^1 + (10258,0)x^2 + (8872,0)x^3 + (3892,0)x^4
2    (3692,0)x^0 + (486,0)x^1 + (7296,0)x^0 + (-4666,0)x^3
3    (997,0)x^0 + (102,0)x^1 + (1863,0)x^2 + (350,0)x^3 + (1496,0)x^4
4      + (1639,0)x^5 + (1469,0)x^6 + (517,0)x^7
```

Listing 3.22: Output of test case for modulo multiplication

The source code is rich on test cases. For details about the functionality of the class `Polynomial`, see the other test cases in the source code.

71

3.9.2. Values of $j(\tau)$

Computing $j(\tau)$ is based on the following formulae.

$$j(\tau) = \frac{(256f(\tau)+1)^3}{f(\tau)}, \tag{3.21}$$

$$f(\tau) = \frac{\Delta(2\tau)}{\Delta(\tau)}, \tag{3.22}$$

$$\Delta(\tau) = q\left(1+\sum_{n\geq 1}(-1)^n\left(q^{\frac{n(3n-1)}{2}}+q^{\frac{n(3n+1)}{2}}\right)\right)^{24}, \tag{3.23}$$

$$q = e^{2i\pi\tau} = cos(2\pi\tau)+isin(2\pi\tau). \tag{3.24}$$

All this formulae are implemented in class `HilbertClassPolynomial`. The following listing shows the implementation of the function $j(\tau)$.

```
 1    public Complex computeJ(BigInteger a, BigInteger b,
 2                            BigInteger D, Context ctx) {
 3      Complex one = new Complex(BigDecimal.ONE, BigDecimal.ZERO, ctx);
 4      Complex two = new Complex(BigDecimal.valueOf(2.0), BigDecimal.ZERO, ctx);
 5      Complex twofivesix = new Complex(BigDecimal.valueOf(256.0),
 6                                       BigDecimal.ZERO, ctx);
 7      BigDecimal re = new BigDecimal(b.negate()).
 8          divide( BigDecimal.valueOf(2).
 9          multiply(new BigDecimal(a), ctx.getMc()),
10                                 ctx.getMc());
11      BigDecimal im = squareRootBig.sqrtBigDecimal(
12                    new BigDecimal(D.abs()), ctx).
13                    divide(BigDecimal.valueOf(2).
14                    multiply(new BigDecimal(a), ctx.getMc()), ctx.getMc()
15                );
16      Complex tau = new Complex(re, im, ctx);
17      Complex deltaTau = computeDeltaTau(tau, ctx);
18      Complex delta2Tau = computeDeltaTau(two.multiply(tau), ctx);
19      Complex fTau = delta2Tau.divide(deltaTau);
20      Complex j1 = twofivesix.multiply(fTau).add(one);
21      Complex j2 = j1.pow(Const.THREE);
22      Complex j = (j2.divide(fTau));
23      return j;
24    }
```

Listing 3.23: Method computeJ in class HilbertClassPolynomial

The functions $f(\tau)$ is directly computed in method `computeJ`. The method $\Delta(\tau)$ is a separate method and is called `computeDeltaTau`. The following listing show the implementaion of `computeDeltaTau`.

```
1   public Complex computeDeltaTau(Complex tau, Context ctx) {
2     Complex zQ = computeQ(tau, ctx);
3     Complex zOne = new Complex(BigDecimal.ONE, BigDecimal.ZERO, ctx);
4     Complex zRes = new Complex(BigDecimal.ZERO, BigDecimal.ZERO, ctx);
5
6     for (Integer n=1; n <= REPEAT; n++) {
7       Integer nMinus = n*(3*n-1)/2;
8       Integer nPlus = n*(3*n+1)/2;
9       Complex sign = new Complex( BigDecimal.valueOf(Math.pow(-1.0, n)),
10                        BigDecimal.ZERO, ctx);
11      zRes = zRes.add(sign.multiply(zQ.pow(BigInteger.valueOf(nMinus)).
12                   add(zQ.pow(BigInteger.valueOf(nPlus)))));
13    }
14    zRes = zQ.multiply((zOne.add(zRes)).pow(BigInteger.valueOf(24)));
15    return zRes;
16  }
```

Listing 3.24: Method computeDeltaTau in class HilbertClassPolynomial

The constant value REPEAT is kind of control parameter which determines the accuracy of the value $\Delta(\tau)$. We have experienced sufficient results by setting REPEAT=50.

The method computeQ computes the value for q. This method is the only place, where we use an GNU-based external open source library to compute the trigonometric functions *sin* and *cos* and as well the exponential function[32].

```
1   public Complex computeQ(Complex tau, Context ctx) {
2     Apfloat t1 = new Apfloat(tau.getRe(), ctx.getPrecision());
3     Apfloat t2 = new Apfloat(tau.getIm(), ctx.getPrecision());
4     Apfloat pi = ApfloatMath.pi(ctx.getPrecision());
5     Apfloat f = ApfloatMath.exp(
6         new Apfloat(-2)
7         .multiply(pi)
8         .multiply(t2)
9     );
10    Apfloat re =ApfloatMath.cos(
11        new Apfloat(2)
12        .multiply(pi)
13        .multiply(t1)
14    );
15    Apfloat im =ApfloatMath.sin(
16        new Apfloat(2)
17        .multiply(pi)
18        .multiply(t1)
19    );
20    Complex zQ = new Complex(
21        new BigDecimal(f.multiply(re).toString()),
22        new BigDecimal(f.multiply(im).toString()), ctx);
23    return zQ;
24  }
```

Listing 3.25: Method computeQ in class HilbertClassPolynomial

---

[32]See http://www.apfloat.org/apfloat_java/ ,downloaded on 06/11/2011

3.9.3. Implementation of Hilbert class polynomial

With the methods from the last section we are ready to implement the Algorithm 7.6.1 from [10], page 415.

```
1    /*
2     * Based on Henri Cohen's book
3     * A Course in Computational Algebraic Number Theory
4     * Section 7.6.2, Algorithm 7.6.1, page 415.
5     */
6    public Polynomial compute(BigInteger discriminant, Context ctx) {
7      // Initialize
8      List<PolynomialComponent> c1 = new ArrayList<PolynomialComponent>();
9      c1.add(new PolynomialComponent(BigInteger.valueOf(0),
10         new Complex(BigDecimal.ONE, BigDecimal.ZERO, ctx)));
11     Polynomial P = new Polynomial(c1, ctx);
12     BigInteger D = discriminant;
13     BigInteger b = D.mod(Const.TWO);
14     BigInteger r =  squareRootBig.sqrtBigInteger(D.abs().
15                          divide(Const.THREE), ctx);
16     while (b.compareTo(r) == -1 || b.compareTo(r) == 0) {
17       BigInteger m = b.pow(2).subtract(D).divide(Const.FOUR);
18       for (BigInteger a=b.max(Const.ONE);
19           // Initialize a
20            a.pow(2).compareTo(m) == -1 || a.pow(2).compareTo(m) == 0;
21          // Loop on a
22            a = a.add(Const.ONE) ) {
23          // Test
24         if (m.mod(a).compareTo(Const.ZERO) == 0) {
25           BigInteger c = m.divide(a);
26           // Compute the j-function
27           Complex j = computeJ(a,b,D, ctx);
28           if (   b.compareTo(a) == 0
29              || c.compareTo(a) == 0
30              || b.compareTo(Const.ZERO) == 0) {
31              // P=P*(X-j)
32              P = p1(P, j, ctx);
33           } else {
34              // P=P*(X^2-2*Re(j)+|j|^2)
35              P = p2(P, j, ctx);
36           }
37         }
38       }
39       // Loop on b
40       b = b.add(Const.TWO);
41     }
42     List<PolynomialComponent> component = P.getComponent();
43     for (int i = 0; i < component.size(); i++) {
44       // Round coefficients
45       component.get(i).setCoefficient(
46             roundCoeff(component.get(i).getCoefficient(), ctx));
47     }
48     P.setComponent(component);
```

```
49      return P;
50    }
```

Listing 3.26: Method compute in class HilbertClassPolynomial

The methods p1 and p2 are responsible to build the Hilbert class polynomial. There, we are using the method modMultiply from class Polynomial.

```
1    // P=P*(X-j)
2    private Polynomial p1(Polynomial P, Complex j, Context ctx) {
3        List<PolynomialComponent> cP1 = new ArrayList<PolynomialComponent>();
4        cP1.add(new PolynomialComponent(BigInteger.valueOf(0),
5                        new Complex(j.getRe().negate(),
6                                    j.getIm().negate(), ctx)));
7        cP1.add(new PolynomialComponent(BigInteger.valueOf(1),
8                        new Complex(BigDecimal.ONE,
9                                    BigDecimal.ZERO, ctx)));
10       Polynomial p1 = new Polynomial(cP1, ctx);
11       P = P.modMultiply(p1, Const.ZERO);
12       return P;
13   }
14
15   // P=P*(X^2-2*Re(j)+|j|^2)
16   private Polynomial p2(Polynomial P, Complex j, Context ctx) {
17       List<PolynomialComponent> cP2 = new ArrayList<PolynomialComponent>();
18       cP2.add(new PolynomialComponent(BigInteger.valueOf(0),
19                        new Complex(j.abs().pow(2), BigDecimal.ZERO, ctx)));
20       cP2.add(new PolynomialComponent(BigInteger.valueOf(1),
21                        new Complex(BigDecimal.valueOf(-2).multiply(j.getRe()),
22                                    BigDecimal.ZERO, ctx)));
23       cP2.add(new PolynomialComponent(BigInteger.valueOf(2),
24                        new Complex(BigDecimal.ONE,
25                                    BigDecimal.ZERO, ctx)));
26       Polynomial p2 = new Polynomial(cP2, ctx);
27       P = P.modMultiply(p2, Const.ZERO);
28       return P;
29   }
```

Listing 3.27: Method p1 and p2 in class HilbertClassPolynomial

3.9.4. Precision of the coefficients of $H_D(x)$

The final coefficients of $H_D(x)$ must be computed within an error of 0.5 at most. A practical estimation is recommended by [10], page 416. The computation of the j values should be done with at least

$$k = \frac{\pi\sqrt{|D|}}{ln(10)} \sum \frac{1}{a} + 10 \qquad (3.25)$$

significant digits.

For a given (fundamendal) discriminant D, we compute a list of reduced binary quadratic forms which belong to the equivalence classes $\mathcal{C}(D)$.

An implementation of the Formula 3.25 loops over the elements (a_i, b_i, c_i) of $\mathcal{C}(D)$ and computes the minimum number of digits k. This integer value is than set in the class `Context` and passed to the `compute` method of class `HilbertClassPolynomial`.

The following listing shows the method `computePrecision` in class `HilbertClassPolynomial`.

```
public int computePrecision(BigInteger D,
                            List<BinaryQuadraticForm> bqfList) {
  double aSum = 0.0;
  for (BinaryQuadraticForm binaryQuadraticForm : bqfList) {
    aSum = aSum + 1/binaryQuadraticForm.getA().doubleValue();
  }
  int prec = (int) (Math.floor(Math.PI
      * Math.sqrt(Math.abs(D.doubleValue())) / Math.log(10)
      * aSum) + 10.0);
  return prec;
}
```

Listing 3.28: Method computePrecision in class HilbertClassPolynomial

3.9.5. Test cases and Hilbert class polynomial data container

The following test case computes the Hilbert class polynomial for the fundamental discriminants in the interval $[-30, 0]$.

```
@Test
public void testCompute() throws Exception {
  List<BigInteger> fdList = fundamentalDiscriminant.
          fundamentalDiscriminants(BigInteger.valueOf(-30),
                                   BigInteger.valueOf(1));
  for (BigInteger d : fdList) {
    List<BinaryQuadraticForm> bqfList = reducedForms.
                              qfList(d, new Context());
    int prec = hilbertClassPolynomial.computePrecision(d, bqfList);
    log.info("Fundamental discriminant: " + d + "  " +
                              "Precision: " + prec );
    Context ctx = new Context(prec);
    Polynomial p = hilbertClassPolynomial.compute(d, ctx);
    p.show();
    log.info("------------------------------------------------");
  }
```

Listing 3.29: Test case computing Hilbert class polynomial

The result is as follows:

```
Fundamental discriminant: -3  Precision: 12
(0,0)x^0 + (1,0)x^1
------------------------------------------------
```

76

```
 4  Fundamental discriminant: -4   Precision: 12
 5  (-1728,0)x^0 + (1,0)x^1
 6  -----------------------------------------------
 7  Fundamental discriminant: -7   Precision: 13
 8  (3375,0)x^0 + (1,0)x^1
 9  -----------------------------------------------
10  Fundamental discriminant: -8   Precision: 13
11  (-8000,0)x^0 + (1,0)x^1
12  -----------------------------------------------
13  Fundamental discriminant: -11   Precision: 14
14  (32768,0)x^0 + (1,0)x^1
15  -----------------------------------------------
16  Fundamental discriminant: -15   Precision: 17
17  (-121287375,0)x^0 + (191025,0)x^1 + (1,0)x^2
18  -----------------------------------------------
19  Fundamental discriminant: -19   Precision: 15
20  (884736,0)x^0 + (1,0)x^1
21  -----------------------------------------------
22  Fundamental discriminant: -20   Precision: 19
23  (-681472000,0)x^0 + (-1264000,0)x^1 + (1,0)x^2
24  -----------------------------------------------
25  Fundamental discriminant: -23   Precision: 23
26  (12771880859375,0)x^0 + (-5151296875,0)x^1 + (3491750,0)x^2 + (1,0)x^3
27  -----------------------------------------------
28  Fundamental discriminant: -24   Precision: 20
29  (14670139392,0)x^0 + (-4834944,0)x^1 + (1,0)x^2
30  -----------------------------------------------
```

Listing 3.30: Hilbert class polynomial for fundamental discriminants in some interval

For large class numbers $h(D)$ the time to compute the Hilbert class polynomial increases vastly[33]. With another test case, we computed the Hilbert class polynomial for $D = -4291$. The coefficients of the resulting Hilbert class polynomial are very large and its degree is 12. The output shows also the reduced binary quadratic forms.

```
 1  D: -4291
 2  (1, 1, 1073)
 3  (29, 1, 37)
 4  (29, -1, 37)
 5  (5, 3, 215)
 6  (5, -3, 215)
 7  (25, 3, 43)
 8  (25, -3, 43)
 9  (13, 5, 83)
10  (13, -5, 83)
11  (7, 7, 155)
12  (31, 7, 35)
13  (31, -7, 35)
14  (964085153313674485822778052799073953536426558892056120622299510
15  138877315361151624483370740312825913834221591708114350297390202420
16  8997376021931461735390870464890404897554432,0)x^0 + (-253573317168
```

---

[33]See [13], page 361.

```
17   1836275131381032549258032549034977111801217759288164330940818378240
18   0595684715420517835895990811323003984277937752796608444525847090640
19   44204799753476581105860608,0)x^1 + (27110604607048319402176904388150
20   34308914555313190114344263978905944370822222686537954720813014973850
21   19894458149056799685092460195359831616743757464516067073157075036050
22   12544,0)x^2 + (-149896319635509786836774376899681344165897202418020
23   5517841300335200631238651162963313644762429016809820659040895260400
24   409789536916084064778641699911418434780464676864,0)x^3 + (4501150700
25   00470448513244972694486970427301530797976203310865546071352943879650
26   18807519106263214430406360133954216992359969966798732841637521372250
27   50954872903971110912,0)x^4 + (-6961715270716475388027688731555895000
28   71900274445693142097588893283911182843673760983062324547370728013550
29   1333295365309076999420138317959966351126372710508134400,0)x^5 + 0000
30   (43916458817966470791097108766632338444878240546707689515866506400060
31   6543136762777526569332773931548572889446962485676560538314861277850
32   5462091805507452928,0)x^6 + (-416078097592946519919580234995707560
33   77750972726638747659222271575586148669620282552625757347791588834250
34   611978184978538804449591702469826264327782 4,0)x^7 + (779878453891650
35   90984350485763658369805513415079080328761206538213340424425858765950
36   627689204053155725341494912073113677958768757491464740536 32,0)x^850
37   + (1331217774815368994460677130544417524268876828172331771798697253
38   16599122137760478951949637571154316555767148094026292932902912,0)x^9
39   + (10974188891854281646830222474964503729835832604907037985301038778
40   7675775958272919188988319588998666549985280,0)x^10 + (23684387081950
41   515092944768872712966479959117936978188817194827574048544128721486500
42   619450343424,0)x^11 + (1,0)x^12
```

Listing 3.31: Hilbert class polynomial with fundamental discriminants D

For curve construction, the Hilbert class polynomials with an upper limit of class number 20 and for fundamental discriminants from -4 to -50000 will be precomputed and *serialized* as Map<Integer, List<HcpContainer>>. The *key* value is an integer and represents the class number $h(D)$. The *value* is a list of HcpContainer. The map is ordered ascending by class number and the list of HcpContainer is ordered ascending by fundamental discriminant. The following listing shows HcpContainer.

```
 1   public class HcpContainer implements Serializable {
 2     private Integer classNumber;
 3     private BigInteger fundamentalDiscriminant;
 4     private List<BinaryQuadraticForm> binaryQuadraticFormList;
 5     private Polynomial hilbertClassPolynomial;
 6
 7     public Integer getClassNumber() {
 8       return classNumber;
 9     }
10     public void setClassNumber(Integer classNumber) {
11       this.classNumber = classNumber;
12     }
13     public BigInteger getFundamentalDiscriminant() {
14       return fundamentalDiscriminant;
15     }
16     public void setFundamentalDiscriminant(BigInteger fundamentalDiscriminant) {
17       this.fundamentalDiscriminant = fundamentalDiscriminant;
```

```
18    }
19    public List<BinaryQuadraticForm> getBinaryQuadraticFormList() {
20      return binaryQuadraticFormList;
21    }
22    public void setBinaryQuadraticFormList(
23      List<BinaryQuadraticForm> binaryQuadraticFormList) {
24      this.binaryQuadraticFormList = binaryQuadraticFormList;
25    }
26    public Polynomial getHilbertClassPolynomial() {
27      return hilbertClassPolynomial;
28    }
29    public void setHilbertClassPolynomial(Polynomial hilbertClassPolynomial) {
30      this.hilbertClassPolynomial = hilbertClassPolynomial;
31    }
32  }
```

Listing 3.32: Class HcpContainer

Number of Hilbert class polynomials per class number is shown in table 3.1.

Class number	Number of Hilbert class polynomials
1	9
2	18
3	16
4	54
5	25
6	51
7	31
8	131
9	34
11	41
12	206
13	37
14	95
15	68
17	45
16	322
19	47
18	150
20	347

Table 3.1.: Number of Hilbert class polynomials per class number

3.10. Implementation of elliptic curves construction with CM-method

For the fundamental discriminants $D < -4$ there are always two elliptic curves, this is the elliptic curve and its quadratic twist[34] by quadratic non-residue. With Theorem 2.1.2 we have a rule to compute the twist of an elliptic curve.

If $D = -3$ there are six isomorphism classes and if $D = -4$ there are four isomorphism classes. These cases will be not considered here, for details see [10], page 472 or [13] Algorithm 7.5.9 page 362.

We sketch the implementation for constructing the elliptic curve with CM for $D < -4$. Input parameter is a probable prime number q.

i) Find a random quadratic non-residue $g \pmod{q}$. This is necessary for computing the twisted curve. See Theorem 2.1.2.

```
1    private BigInteger findRandomQuadraticNonResidue(BigInteger q) {
2        BigInteger g = legendre.randomQuadraticNonResidue(q);
3      return g;
4    }
```

ii) Find a *suitable* fundamental discriminant $D < -4$ with algorithm described in Section 3.4.

```
1    fundamentalDiscriminant.isFundamentalDiscriminant(D)
```

iii) Determine f and t of equation $4q = t^2 + f^2 D$ with modified Cornacchia algorithm described in Section 3.7. This step gives the *order* of the elliptic curve and the next steps determine the parameters of the elliptic curve. The connection between determining the order of the elliptic curve and identifying the elliptic curve parameters is given since we are using for both steps the same fundamental discriminant.

```
1    ModifiedCornacchiaResult mcr = modifiedCornacchia.calc(q, D, ctx);
```

iv) Identitfy the precision for computing the Hilbert class polynomial with Formula 3.25.

```
1    // Compute the reduced binary quadratic form
2    // for a given fundamental discriminant.
3    List<BinaryQuadraticForm> bqfList =
4                       reducedForms.qfList(D, new Context());
5    int prec = hilbertClassPolynomial.computePrecision(D, bqfList);
6    Context ctx = new Context(prec);
```

v) Compute the Hilbert class polynomial with algorithm described in Section 3.9.3.

```
1    Polynomial hcp = hilbertClassPolynomial.compute(D, ctx);
```

vi) Obtain the roots $j \in \mathbb{F}_q$ of Hilbert class polynomial.

---

[34]This is depending on the choice of trace of Frobenius t or $-t$.

```
1    Polynomial hcp = hilbertClassPolynomial.modReduction(q);
2    List<Complex> jList = hcp.modRoots(q);
```

vii) Build the elliptic curve and its quadratic twist with Formula 2.8 and Theorem 2.1.2 for one root *j* obtained from the previous step. The two elliptic curves are collected in the data container list ecContainerList.

```
1    List<ECContainer> ecContainerList =
2                new ArrayList<ECContainer>();
3    for (Complex complex : jList) {
4      BigInteger j = complex.getRe().toBigInteger();
5      // c=j/(j-1728)
6      BigInteger c = fo.divide(j,
7          fo.subtract(j, BigInteger.valueOf(1728)));
8      // Create Weierstrass object.
9      WeierstrassAffine ec = new WeierstrassAffine();
10     // a1=-3*c, b1=2*c
11     BigInteger a1 = fo.multiply(Const.THREE.negate(), c);
12     BigInteger b1 = fo.multiply(Const.TWO, c);
13     // Initialize the Weierstrass curve ec with a1 and b1
14     ec.init(a1, b1, q);
15     Point point = ec.randomPoint();
16     Point pointRes1 = ec.multiply(point, o1);
17     Point pointRes2 = ec.multiply(point, o2);
18     // Check which order belongs to ec.
19     if (pointRes1.equals(ec.getIdentity())) {
20       ecContainerList.add(new ECContainer(ec, o1));
21     } else if (pointRes2.equals(ec.getIdentity())) {
22       ecContainerList.add(new ECContainer(ec, o2));
23     }
24     // Build the twisted curve in the same manner.
25     // a2=-3*c*q^2, b1=2*c*q^3
26     BigInteger a2 = fo.multiply(fo.multiply(
27         Const.THREE.negate(), c),fo.pow(g, Const.TWO));
28     BigInteger b2 = fo.multiply(fo.multiply(Const.TWO, c),
29                         fo.pow(g, Const.THREE));
30     // Initialize the Weierstrass curve ec with a2 and b2
31     // Create Weierstrass object.
32     WeierstrassAffine ecTwisted = new WeierstrassAffine();
33     ecTwisted.init(a2, b2, q);
34     Point pointTwisted = ecTwisted.randomPoint();
35     Point pointTwistedRes1 =
36                 ecTwisted.multiply(pointTwisted, o1);
37     Point pointTwistedRes2 =
38                 ecTwisted.multiply(pointTwisted, o2);
39     // Check if the two elliptic curves
40     // really fits with the order
41     if (pointTwistedRes1.equals(ecTwisted.getIdentity())) {
42       ecContainerList.add(new ECContainer(ecTwisted, o1));
43     } else if (pointTwistedRes2.equals(
44                     ecTwisted.getIdentity())) {
45       ecContainerList.add(new ECContainer(ecTwisted, o2));
46     }
```

81

```
47          }
```

Note, that this algorithm is consuming the elliptic curve arithmetic system from the first chapter, as ist uses the class `WeierstrassAffine`.

We improve this algorithm by precomputing the Hilbert class polynomials (Section 3.9.5). With the method `revokeHcpContainer` we deserialize the data container with precomputed Hilbert class polynomials and get the map `Map<Integer, List<HcpContainer>>`. The keys of the map are the class numbers. For each class number (up to 20 are precomputed[35]), we get a list `List<HcpContainer>`. Each entry of this list contains the fundamental discriminant, the list of binary quadratic forms and the Hilbert class polynomial. This list is sorted ascending by fundamental discriminant, like described in Section 3.9.5.

The following listing is the controller method which generates the elliptic curves. The method `revokeHcpContainer` *deserializes* the precomputed Hilbert class polynomials. We stop the loop over the class numbers respectively the fundamental discriminants as soon as we get a list `List<ECContainer>` with two elliptic curves, i.e. the curve and its quadratic twist. That is, the first root modulo q of the Hilbert class polynomial is sufficient to get two elliptic curves.

```
1    public List<ECContainer> generate(BigInteger q) {
2      fo.init(q);
3      BigInteger g = findRandomQuadraticNonResidue(q);
4      // Deserialize the data container with
5      // precomputed Hilbert class polynomials
6      Map<Integer, List<HcpContainer>> mapHcpContainer
7                            = revokeHcpContainer();
8      Set<Integer> setClassNumber = mapHcpContainer.keySet();
9      List<ECContainer> ecContainerList = new ArrayList<ECContainer>();
10     // Loop over class number
11     for (Integer cn : setClassNumber) {
12       if (ecContainerList.size() == 2) {
13         break;
14       }
15       List<HcpContainer> hcList = mapHcpContainer.get(cn);
16       BigInteger fd = Const.ZERO;
17       for (HcpContainer hc : hcList) {
18         if (ecContainerList.size() == 2) {
19           break;
20         }
21         fd = hc.getFundamentalDiscriminant();
22         Polynomial hp = hc.getHilbertClassPolynomial();
23         // if there are solutions then there are always two
24         ecContainerList = generate(q,fd,hp,g);
25       }
26     }
27     return ecContainerList;
28   }
```

---

[35]Therefore, the maximal degree of the precomputed Hilbert class polynomials is 20.

The generate method with the four parameter at the end of this method is responsible for delivering the elliptic curves as a list. The method is basically the steps iii), vi), vii) of the sketched implementation described at the beginning of this section.

The following test case generates an elliptic curve for a random probable prime number with 200 to 300 digits.

```
1   @Test
2   public void testECGenerator01() throws Exception {
3     BigInteger start = new BigInteger("10").pow(200);
4     BigInteger end = new BigInteger("10").pow(300);
5     // Generate a random probable prime number
6     // with 200 to 300 digits.
7     BigInteger q = randomInteger.nextRandomBigInteger
8                        (start,end).nextProbablePrime();
9     log.info("q: " + q);
10    List<ECContainer> ecContainerList = ecGenerator.generate(q);
11    show(ecContainerList);
12  }
```

Listing 3.33: Constructing an elliptic curve for a random prime number

```
1   q: 236438491444701656161946852154232258098792503652
2       524738102870537011332377863959773134041000203111572
3       200940769871170781328938632151100527128132664397094
4       995016514041785099351520787973365410546436811954143
5       748990333120241972010075624727258775566920506000820
6       035543184520667674572615644465648122918537668749
7   Classnumber: 2
8   Fundamental discriminant: -20
9   Hilbert class polynomial: (14670139392,0)x^0 + (-4834944,0)x^1 + (1,0)x^2
10  y^2 = x^3 + 12313209873116386966639816975326469506785236920
11             439965856785349099553671526394877654710315294 58
12             010848140974510270435379393063828398034011185 52
13             665718824034546990780124851144354043300028896 75
14             589841096917531421774010799147531535237231122 92
15             570246215985221430888913012111227220156417674 0
16             732175281376882973*x + 1621695022743297008126 19
17             755412020193147884778001291981347561868499233 41
18             126652682563081067523407171570237908871847544 94
19             263048041702094750252476940528135342037642425 23
20             251117713445195939554565783232286060991192587 96
21             331661076559154341274321755854471878790127872 88
22             543099309852225343346156346932537604612 93
23  with order 236438491444701656161946852154232258098792503652
24             5247381028705370113323778639597731340410002031 11
25             5722009407698711707813289386321511005271281326 6
26             4397094022729085257392836693407042033427722700 0
27             7397068662572931050736438908723856460881415727 8
28             9744033071750807299286021692729775169088162779 5
29             3250750181092454
30  twist:
31  y^2 = x^3 + 11001120927715337442829280817388782679753020 66
```

```
32              73714741296898932798748098422362744833200117 18
33              85323201217044038415629701804391830660976529 25
34              25940630204921209490203538914805859297284450 63
35              66575515134232338729487272944064722156033762 82
36              61717794597970542025287769149983914209374399 83
37              41476542345597860458 1020*x + 77761785306548700
38              91042399679362247605363457028263414116841755 89
39              37322324227781316509005952521054677016367984 41
40              75247757249955290680757956076797091655521764 25
41              36451125165009679177250858912727530707052958 70
42              80374950918260825711989658741726322733291420 76
43              47918556706735198902547293171393601437580237 7
44              1806139
45 with order 2364384914447016561619468521542322580987925036 52
46              52473810287053701133237786395977313404100020311 1
47              57220094076987117078132893863215110052712813266 4
48              39709596730394282617736200963453391330309839279 9
49              65322166176867015887609485678158664064036027215 9
50              43770482655934115776687206237162832247265334299 5
51              086894245046
```

Listing 3.34: Output of the test case for random prime number

3.11. Constructing elliptic curves of prescribed order

Constructing elliptic curves of prescribed order is more difficult than constructing elliptic curves for a given prime q. Based on the known equations

$$
\begin{aligned}
\#E &= q + 1 - t \text{ and} \\
D &= t^2 - 4q,
\end{aligned}
$$

we express D (any discriminant not necessarily the fundamental discriminant) with

$$
D = (q + 1 - \#E)^2 - 4q. \tag{3.26}
$$

If we get D for some given $\#E$ and q in the set of precomputed interval, everthing is fine. But it is easy to verify experimentally that D is mainly out of the expected interval. Therefore, we need to compute the Hilbert class polynomial *online* during the CM-method algorithm. This is not efficient (or impossible) since with increasing D, the time to compute the Hilbert class polynomial increases[36] rapidly.

For a detailed treatment of constructing elliptic curves of prescribed order with CM-method see Reinier Bröker's PhD-Thesis [8].

---

[36]See [8], Chapter 3.

For the sake of completeness, we will give an implementation of a naive method for constructing elliptic curves of prescribed order, which is probabilistic and not based on CM-method. The algorithm to this implementation is also based on Reinier Bröker's work[37].

We choose a prime q from Hasse interval and construct random curves over $\mathbb{F}_q$ until the correct curve is identified or the number of tries reach an upper limit.

Input is an integer $N > 4$. Output is an elliptic curve E over $\mathbb{F}_q$ with q in Hasse interval and $\#E(\mathbb{F}_q) = N$.

In the first part of the algorithm we loop from $N + 1 - \sqrt{N}$ to $N + 1 + \sqrt{N}$ and search for a prime number. If there is a prime q, we compute $t = q + 1 - N$.

```
1   public EllipticCurveInterface generateNaiveWithPrescribedOrder
2                                            (BigInteger N) {
3       Context ctx = new Context();
4       SquareRootBig squareRootBig = new SquareRootBig();
5       // N+1-sqrt(N)
6       BigInteger start = N.add(Const.ONE).
7               subtract(squareRootBig.sqrtBigInteger(N, ctx));
8       // N+1+sqrt(N)
9       BigInteger end = N.add(Const.ONE).
10              add(squareRootBig.sqrtBigInteger(N, ctx));
11      BigInteger t = Const.ZERO;
12      BigInteger q = start;
13      for (; q.compareTo(end) == -1; q = q.add(Const.ONE) ) {
14        if (q.isProbablePrime(3)) {
15          // t=q+1-N
16          t = q.add(Const.ONE).subtract(N);
17          break;
18        }
19      }
20      ...
```

Listing 3.35: First part of naive elliptic curve search algorithm

In the second part we pick a random element b from interval $[3, q]$ and initialize the elliptic curve

$$y^2 = x^3 + bx - b. \tag{3.27}$$

We repeat this step until the elliptic curve satisfies the condition that it fits to the t obtained from the first part or an upper limit of repeat steps is reached.

```
1       ...
2       for (int i=1; i<10000; i++) {
3         // get a random element from [3,q]
4         BigInteger b = randomInteger.nextRandomBigInteger(Const.THREE,q);
5         Weierstrass wCurve = new WeierstrassAffine();
6         // Initialize y^2=x^3+bx-b
7         wCurve.init(b, b.negate(), q);
```

---

[37]See [8], page 18.

```
8      // Check if curve is an elliptic curve
9      if (wCurve.isNonSingular()) {
10       // point = (1,1)
11       Point point = new Point(Const.ONE, Const.ONE, Const.ONE);
12       // k = q+1-t
13       BigInteger k = q.add(Const.ONE).subtract(t);
14       if (wCurve.multiply(point, k).equals(wCurve.getIdentity())) {
15         // u = q+1-k
16         BigInteger u = q.add(Const.ONE).subtract(k);
17         if (u.compareTo(t)==0) {
18           return wCurve;
19         }
20       }
21       k = q.add(Const.ONE).add(t);
22       if (t.compareTo(Const.ZERO) != 0 && wCurve.multiply(point, k).
23                                  equals(wCurve.getIdentity())) {
24         // u = q+1-k
25         BigInteger u = k.subtract(q).subtract(Const.ONE);
26         if (u.compareTo(t.negate())==0) {
27           // twist curve
28           return wCurve;
29         }
30       }
31     }
32   }
33   return null;
```

Listing 3.36: Second part of naive elliptic curve search algorithm

The following test case show the usage of the method `generateNaiveWithPrescribedOrder`.

```
1    @Test
2    public void testECGeneratorWithPrescribedOrder() throws Exception {
3      BigInteger start = new BigInteger("10").pow(6);
4      BigInteger end = new BigInteger("10").pow(8);
5      BigInteger N = randomInteger.nextRandomBigInteger(start,end).
6                          nextProbablePrime();
7      log.info("N: " + N);
8      EllipticCurveInterface ec =
9            ecGenerator.generateNaiveWithPrescribedOrder(N);
10     if (ec != null) {
11       ec.show();
12     } else {
13       log.info("No curve found!");
14     }
15   }
```

Listing 3.37: Test case of naive elliptic curve search algorithm

```
1  N: 17270359
2  q: 17266211
3  t: -4147
4  y^2 = x^3 + 16835530*x + 430681
```

86

Listing 3.38: Output of the test case

3.12. Conclusion to chapter construction of elliptic curves with CM

In this chapter, we discussed three approaches of constructing an elliptic curve over a finite field and identifying its order.

1. Random curve generation and point counting.

2. Constructing of an elliptic curve for a given prime q (CM-method).

3. Constructing of an elliptic curve of prescribed order.

The first and the third approach were more a proof of concept than a profound treatment. The second approach is implemented completly. That is, with the second approach we are able to construct elliptic curves over an finite field $\mathbb{F}_q$ for a given prime number q with up to 900 digits.

The difficulties in deploying the CM-method is mainly the computation of the Hilbert class polynomial. Hilbert class polynomial needs a high precision computation and therefore computing it as needed (*online*) is not practical.

An improvement is a precomputation of Hilbert class polynomials for a specified interval of fundamental discriminants, which was realized in this chapter for $D \in [-50000, -4]$.

In the next chapter we introduce and implement two similar primality proving algorithms based on elliptic curves. Especially Atkin-Morain's algorithm, which is an improvement of Goldwasser-Kilian's algorithm will be an application of constructing of elliptic curves based on CM-method.

Chapter 4.

Elliptic curve primality proving

Proving the primality of a number by algorithms based on elliptic curves are called *elliptic curve primality proving* algorithms (ECPP). The basic idea of ECPP is the same like other primality proving algorithms, that is finding a group and showing its order is a prime. A significant property of primality proving algorithms is that they generate a *certificate*. With the certificate it is possible to repeat the proof anytime from someone else. In the case of ECPP, the certificate is called the *Atkin-Goldwasser-Kilian-Morain certificate*, named after the main developers of ECPP. The generation of the certificate happens during the *down-run procedure*.

For a given probable prime N_0, the method of primality proving delivers a new number N_1. For N_1, we also assume that it is a probable prime and apply again the method of primality proving and get a new probable prime N_2. This procedure carries on, until N_i is small enough so that we are certain about the primality of N_i, that is if N_i is prime then N_0 is prime. The total sum of all these steps is the mentioned down-run procedure. Each down-run procedure step gives us a set of information beside N_i, so that we can repeat the proving process. Hence, the collection of the sets of information for each step is the mentioned certificate.

In this chapter, we implement the *Goldwasser-Kilian's ECPP algorithm* which uses elliptic curves created by *generating-and-point-counting* method and the *Atkin-Morain's ECPP algorithm* that uses elliptic curves with CM. Atkin-Morain's ECPP algorithm is a improvement of Goldwasser-Kilian's ECPP algorithm.

Before starting with this both algorithms, we discuss the simpler structured *Pocklington-Lehmer test* which is also a primatily proving algorithm that uses the group $\mathbb{Z}_n^\times$ instead of $E(\mathbb{F}_n)$. With Pocklington-Lehmer primality test[38] it is easier to explain the primality proving algorithm. Goldwasser-Kilian's ECPP algorithm will be illustrated as an extension of Pocklington-Lehmer primality test.

4.1. Pocklington-Lehmer primality test

The Pocklington-Lehmer primality test relies on the following

---

[38]Note, although it is called primality *test*, the result is a *proof* of primality of a given number.

Proposition 4.1.1. *Let $n > 1$ be an integer, and let $n - 1 = rs$ with $r > \sqrt{n}$. Suppose that, for each prime $q \mid r$, there exists an integer a_q with*

$$a_q^{n-1} \equiv 1 \pmod{n} \tag{4.1}$$

and

$$gcd(a_q^{\frac{n-1}{q}} - 1, n) = 1. \tag{4.2}$$

For the proof see [30], page 195.

The following example[39] explains descriptively the application of Proposition 4.1.1 and the terms down-run procedure and certificate.

Let $n = 153533$. By factoring $n - 1$ we have $n - 1 = 4 \cdot 131 \cdot 293$. Let $r := 4 \cdot 131 \geq \sqrt{n}$. Obviously 2 is a prime factor of r, and an appropriate $a_q \in \mathbb{N}$ is given by:

$$q = 2 : 2^{n-1} \equiv 1 \pmod{n}, \ gcd(2^{\frac{n-1}{2}} - 1, n) = 1 \Rightarrow a_2 := 2$$

$$q = 131 : 2^{n-1} \equiv 1 \pmod{n}, \ gcd(2^{\frac{n-1}{131}} - 1, n) = 1 \Rightarrow a_{131} := 2$$

Properly speaking, we have to do the same procedure for 2 and 131. Clearly 2 is a prime, for 131 we apply again Pocklington-Lehmer primality test. Hence, for the new $n = 131$, we have $131 - 1 = 2 \cdot 5 \cdot 13 \Rightarrow r := 13 \geq \sqrt{131}$,

$$q = 13 : 2^{n-1} \equiv 1 \pmod{n}, \ gcd(2^{\frac{n-1}{13}} - 1, n) = 1 \Rightarrow a_{13} := 2$$

The down-run procedure is as follows:

We will prove $n = 153533$ and get with Pocklington-Lehmer test a new number 131. Using Pocklington-Lehmer test again for 131, we get 13 and again we get 2.

The Pocklington-Lehmer certificate is the list a_{131}, a_{13} and a_2 and each element of the certificate satisfies the Proposition 4.1.1, which can be quickly checked by another person.

The success of primality proving with Pocklington-Lehmer test is depending on finding enough factors of $n - 1$. Note, that $n - 1$ is the order of the group $\mathbb{Z}_n^\times$. If we can not find factors of $n - 1$, the primality proving is not possible. ECPP which works with the groups $E(\mathbb{F}_n)$ has here an significant advantange compared to Pocklington-Lehmer test, since there are enough choices for the elliptic curve such that we can probably find a number (order of $E(\mathbb{F}_n)$) that can be partially factored. This is the idea of Goldwasser-Kilian's ECPP algorithm, which will be implemented in next section.

---

[39]See [30] page 195.

4.2. Goldwasser-Kilian's ECPP

The Goldwasser-Kilian's ECPP[40] relies on the following

Proposition 4.2.1. *Let n be an integer coprime to 6 and different from 1 and E an elliptic curve over $\mathbb{F}_n$. Assume that we know an integer m and a point $P \in E(\mathbb{F}_n)$ satisfying the following conditions.*

1. *There exist a prime divisor q of m such that*

$$q > \left(\sqrt[4]{n} + 1 \right)^2. \tag{4.3}$$

2. *$mP = O = (0 : 1 : 0)$.*

3. *$\frac{m}{q}P = (x : y : t)$ with $t \in \mathbb{F}_n^*$.*

Then n is prime.

For the proof see [10], page 468.

This proposition is the fundament for ECPP algorithms. In the next sections, we will develop the algorithm for Goldwasser-Kilian's ECPP based on this proposition.

4.2.1. Generation of a random curve

For the algorithm, first we need an elliptic curve over $\mathbb{F}_n$. Goldwasser-Kilian propose to generate a random curve of Weierstraß form and compute its order by counting the points. This is the generating-and-point-counting part of the algorithm. The following class generates[41] an elliptic curve over $\mathbb{F}_n$.

```
1  @Service
2  public class ECGeneratorRandom implements ECGeneratorInterface {
3      @Autowired
4      private RandomInteger randomInteger;
5      @Autowired
6      private ECPointCountLegendre ecPointCountLegendre;
7      @Autowired
8      private FiniteOperator fo;
9      @Override
10     public List<ECContainer> generate(BigInteger n) {
11         List<ECContainer> ecContainerList = new ArrayList<ECContainer>();
12         fo.init(n);
13             BigInteger gcd = Const.ZERO;
14             while ( !(gcd.compareTo(Const.ONE) == 0)) {
15             BigInteger a = randomInteger.nextRandomBigInteger
16                 (Const.ONE, n.subtract(Const.ONE));
```

---

[40]See [17].

[41]We can not use the method `randomCurve` from elliptic curve arithmetic system, since `randomCurve` generates a completly arbitrary curve. Here, we need a curve over $\mathbb{F}_n$.

```
17        BigInteger b = randomInteger.nextRandomBigInteger
18            (Const.ONE, n.subtract(Const.ONE));
19        // A = 4*a^3
20        BigInteger A = fo.multiply(Const.FOUR, fo.pow(a, Const.THREE));
21        // B = 27*b^2
22        BigInteger B = fo.multiply(Const.TWENTYSEVEN,
23                        fo.pow(b, Const.TWO));
24        // check coprime
25        // gcd(n, 4*a^3+27*b^2) = 1
26            gcd = n.gcd(fo.add(A, B));
27            if (gcd.compareTo(Const.ONE) == 0) {
28            WeierstrassAffine ec = new WeierstrassAffine();
29            ec.init(a, b, n);
30            BigInteger order =  ecPointCountLegendre.order(a, b, n);
31            ecContainerList.add(new ECContainer(ec, order));
32            }
33        }
34    return ecContainerList;
35    }
36 }
```

Listing 4.1: Class ECGeneratorRandom

Although we need only one curve, the method `generate` returns a list of `ECContainer` since the implementation of the interface `ECGeneratorInterface` defines this restriction. This is a software architectural effect, since the code for generation of CM-curves from last chapter also implements the interface `ECGeneratorInterface` and there we have the curve and its twist. The method `generation` avoids also curves with bad reduction like described in section 2.4.8.

The order of the curve is computed by method `order` in class `ECPointCountLegendre`, see Listing 3.2. To improve the Goldwasser-Kilian algorithm, this part could be replaced by an algorithm that implements Schoof's algorithm, but this not relevant here, since we are more interested in generating curve with CM-method.

4.2.2. One step of down-run procedure

The proposition 4.2.1 describes one step of the down-run procedure. After generating the curve with its order (data container `ECContainer`), we search for an prime divisor q of the order, denoted by m in Proposition 4.2.1. The prime divisor q is computed by Pollard $p - 1$ algorithm[42]. After having q, we check the criterion

$$q > \left(\sqrt[4]{n} + 1 \right)^2. \qquad (4.4)$$

We call this criterion the *Hasse criterion*[43]. The described steps are repeated until an upper limit of loops are reached or the Hasse criterion is satisfied.

---

[42]See [10], Section 8.8, page 438

[43]Note, this is not a usual name for this criterion and it is only used in this thesis

```java
// upper limit, try 100 times
for (int k=0; k<100; k++) {
    // get a elliptic curve
    ECContainer ecc = ecGenerator.generate(n).get(0);
    // get a factor of the order
    q = pollardPMinusOne.factor(ecc.getOrder(), 100);
    if (!(q.compareTo(Const.ZERO) == 0) &&
                hasseCriterion(ecc.getOrder().divide(q),q,n)) {
        ec = ecc.getEc();
        order = ecc.getOrder();
        // Hasse criterion satisfied
        // exit loop
        break;
    }
}
```

Listing 4.2: Searching for an factor q

The following is the implementation of Hasse criterion.

```java
public boolean hasseCriterion(BigInteger k,
                    BigInteger q, BigInteger n) {
    int prec = bigIntegerToBinary.calc(n, 10).size()*2;
    Context ctx = new Context(prec);
    boolean criterion1 = k.compareTo(Const.ONE) == 1;
    BigDecimal qd = new BigDecimal(q);
    BigDecimal qn = new BigDecimal(n);
    BigDecimal l = squareRootBig.sqrtBigDecimal(qd, ctx).
                    subtract(BigDecimal.ONE).pow(4);
    boolean criterion2 = l.compareTo(qn) == 1;
    return criterion1 && criterion2;
}
```

Listing 4.3: Hasse criterion

If there exists a curve E and a factor q of the $\#E$ then we are searching for a point P on E which satisfies the second and third condition of Proposition 4.2.1.

$$\#EP = O = (0:1:0),$$
$$\frac{\#E}{q}P = (x:y:t).$$

```java
public Point operateOnPoint(BigInteger n, BigInteger q,
    EllipticCurveInterface ec, BigInteger order)
                    throws CompositeException {
    // check second and third condition of
    // Goldwasser-Kilian proposition
    Point U = ec.getIdentity();
    BigInteger orderDivq = order.divide(q);
    Point P = null;
    while (U.equals(ec.getIdentity())) {
```

```
10        P = ec.randomPoint();
11        U = ec.multiply(P, orderDivq);
12      }
13      Point V = ec.multiply(U, q);
14      if (!V.equals(ec.getIdentity())) {
15        throw new RuntimeException(n + " is composite !");
16      }
17      return P;
18    }
```

Listing 4.4: Second and third condition of Goldwasser-Kilian proposition

Finally, the following condition decides, if q is the new value which has to be checked. If so, the next step of down-run procedure starts.

```
1      Point V = ec.multiply(U, q);
2      if (!V.equals(ec.getIdentity())) {
3        throw new RuntimeException(n + " is composite !");
4      }
```

Listing 4.5: Finding a point P

The down-run procedure steps will be repeated until it is obvious that q is a prime or the algorithm will end with the message that n is a composite. For the complete listing see source code of class `GoldwasserKilianECPrimalityProving`.

4.2.3. Certificate

The certificate is a data container which has q, the elliptic curve E, the order $\#E$ and the point P. The structure of the certificate is also valid for Atkin-Morain's ECPP.

```
1    public class Certificate {
2      private BigInteger q;
3      private EllipticCurveInterface ec;
4      private BigInteger order;
5      private Point point;
6      public Certificate(BigInteger q, EllipticCurveInterface ec,
7            BigInteger order, Point point) {...
8      public BigInteger getQ() {...
9      public void setQ(BigInteger q) {...
10     public BigInteger getOrder() {...
11     public void setOrder(BigInteger order) {...
12     public EllipticCurveInterface getEc() {...
13     public void setEc(EllipticCurveInterface ec) {...
14     public Point getPoint() {...
15     public void setPoint(Point point) {...
16   }
```

Listing 4.6: Certificate class

4.2.4. Implementation of Goldwasser-Kilian's ECPP

```
1   public class GoldwasserKilianECPrimalityProving
2                        extends ECPrimalityProving
3                        implements ECPrimalityProvingInterface {
4       ...
5
6       public void primeProve(BigInteger n) {
7           BigInteger primeLimit = new BigInteger("100");
8           // Inialization of class variable certList,
9           // which can be accessed by a getter-method
10          certList = new ArrayList<Certificate>();
11          BigInteger q = prove(n);
12          int step = 1;
13          while (q.compareTo(primeLimit) == 1) {
14            q = prove(q);
15          }
16      }
17
18      public BigInteger prove(BigInteger n) {
19      BigInteger q = Const.ONE;
20      EllipticCurveInterface ec = null;
21      BigInteger order = Const.ZERO;
22      for (int k=0; k<100; k++) {
23        ECContainer ecc = ecGenerator.generate(n).get(0);
24        // Factor with Pollard p-1 (try 100 times)
25        q = pollardPMinusOne.factor(ecc.getOrder(), 100);
26        if (!(q.compareTo(Const.ZERO) == 0) &&
27          hasseCriterion(ecc.getOrder().divide(q),q,n)) {
28          // Hasse criterion valid
29          ec = ecc.getEc();
30          order = ecc.getOrder();
31          break;
32        }
33      }
34      if (ec != null) {
35            Point P = null;
36      try {
37        // check second and third condition of
38        // Goldwasser-Kilian proposition
39        P = operateOnPoint(n, q, ec, order);
40      } catch (CompositeException e) {
41        e.printStackTrace();
42      }
43            certList.add(new Certificate(q, ec, order, P));
44      }
45      return q;
46      }
47  }
```

Listing 4.7: Essential methods of class GoldwasserKilianECPrimalityProving

4.2.5. Test case

The bottleneck in this algorithm is the counting order method. Therefore, the test cases are realized with number up to 6 digits. In the following test case, we prove the primality of 806011.

```
1   @Test
2   public void testProve1() throws Exception {
3       n=BigInteger.valueOf(806011);
4       ecPrimalityProving.primeProve(n);
5   }
```

Listing 4.8: Test case 806011

The resulting certificate is shown in the following listing.

```
1   Integer to prove:806011
2   CERTIFICATE:
3   ===== 1 =====
4   q:      24379
5   P:      (253787,70455,1)
6   EC:     y^2 = x^3 + 599158*x + 132012
7   Order: 804507
8   ===== 2 =====
9   q:      1627
10  P:      (9587,2878,1)
11  EC:     y^2 = x^3 + 13746*x + 7439
12  Order: 24405
13  ===== 3 =====
14  q:      233
15  P:      (413,317,1)
16  EC:     y^2 = x^3 + 1576*x + 376
17  Order: 1631
18  ===== 4 =====
19  q:      31
20  P:      (184,80,1)
21  EC:     y^2 = x^3 + 223*x + 69
22  Order: 248
```

Listing 4.9: Result test case 806011

The interpretation of this certificate is as following: If 31 is prime, then 806011 is prime. Obviously 31 is a prime, therefore 806011 is prime.

4.3. Atkin-Morain's ECPP

In Goldwasser-Kilian's ECPP algorithm the random generation of an elliptic curve and counting the order is not satisfying. This makes the algorithm more of theoretical nature. Using the same basic idea of Proposition 4.2.1, Atkin-Morain's practical approach[44] is to choose elliptic

---
[44]See [20] and [1].

curves with CM instead of random curves. The rest of the primality proof works in the same way like Goldwasser-Kilian's algorithm.

4.3.1. Implementation of Atkin-Morain's ECPP

The primality proving algorithm is implemented in class `AtkinMorainECPrimalityProving`.

```
 1
 2    public class AtkinMorainECPrimalityProving
 3            extends ECPrimalityProving
 4            implements ECPrimalityProvingInterface {
 5      ...
 6
 7      public void primeProve(BigInteger n) {
 8        BigInteger primeLimit = new BigInteger("100");
 9        // Inialization of class variable certList,
10        // which can be accessed by a getter-method
11        certList = new ArrayList<Certificate>();
12        BigInteger q = prove(n);
13        int step = 1;
14        while (q.compareTo(primeLimit) == 1) {
15        q = prove(q);
16        }
17      }
18
19      public BigInteger prove(BigInteger n) {
20        // revoke precomputed Hilbert class polynomials
21        Map<Integer, List<HcpContainer>> mapHcpContainer =
22                    ecGenerator.revokeHcpContainer();
23        // Get the list of class numbers
24        // and fundamental discriminants
25        List<FdCn> fdCnList = ecGenerator.getFdList(mapHcpContainer);
26        BigInteger q = Const.ONE;
27        EllipticCurveInterface ec = null;
28        BigInteger order = Const.ZERO;
29        boolean primefactorFound = false;
30        boolean curveFound = false;
31        // loop over fundamental discriminants
32        for (FdCn fdCn : fdCnList) {
33          if (fdCn.getFd().compareTo(Const.FOUR.negate()) == -1) {
34            List<ECContainer> eccList = ecGenerator.
35                      generate(n, mapHcpContainer, fdCn.getFd());
36            if (eccList.size() > 0) {
37              for (ECContainer ecc : eccList) {
38                curveFound = true;
39                // Factor with Pollard p-1 (try 100 times)
40                q = pollardPMinusOne.factor(ecc.getOrder(), 100);
41                // Checking the Hasse criterion
42                if (!(q.compareTo(Const.ZERO) == 0) &&
43                    hasseCriterion(ecc.getOrder().divide(q),q,n)) {
44                  // Hasse criterion valid
```

96

```
45        ec = ecc.getEc();
46        order = ecc.getOrder();
47        primefactorFound = true;
48        break;
49      } else {
50        // Hasse criterion not valid
51        primefactorFound = false;
52      }
53    }
54  }
55  }
56  if (curveFound && primefactorFound ) break;
57  }
58  // From here Goldwasser-Kilian and
59  // Atkin-Morain are identical
60  if (ec != null) {
61    Point P = null;
62    try {
63      // check second and third condition of
64      // Goldwasser-Kilian proposition
65      P = operateOnPoint(n, q, ec, order);
66    } catch (CompositeException e) {
67      e.printStackTrace();
68    }
69    certList.add(new Certificate(q, ec, order, P));
70  }
71  return q;
72  }
73 }
```

Listing 4.10: Essential methods of class AtkinMorainECPrimalityProving

4.3.2. Test case

For the test case, we will use the number 8182798124355244964627830567604949510629491820276588073002759151574415481374655251823172734091367500. The number has 101 digits (336 bit).

The resulting certificate has 34 down-run-steps. In the following listing we only illustrate first three and the last three.

```
1 Integer to prove:8182798124355244964627830567604949510629491820276588073002
2                   759151574415481374655251823172734091367500
3 CERTIFICATE:
4 ===== 1 =====
5 q:     9091997915950272182919811741783277234032768689196218590004354436332
6        212148057198293567049441456822
7 P:     (6220180849427892041209677511467705115643502748962855162878038502782
8        545285444409155968001327175355700
9        179586074838516782852133894692755227878598606426678892648213695783
10       3864336813504217225222692145934070
```

97

```
11  EC:    y^2 = x^3 + 21032938981503167219284006130559345604728532347969268680
12         24264454120296757897652363444228440459590599*x + 405300281746995216
13         17996199696999343300104425723653107469985663131636079148984668592252 6
14         295290878512670
15  Order: 8182798124355244964627830567604949510629491820276596731003918992699 3
16         590933251478464210344497311139899
17  ===== 2 =====
18  q:     9091997915950272182919811741783277234032768689196371505570607873311 2
19         592300930515938732302507175204 9
20  P:     (25605773418402387580299791666692924584199654237310961891374511778 81
21          350573017966069675213491802584201,4562411530430753590570370376657394 54
22          23585248255487511868420495941590447291655451238988549058500796346 54
23          ,1)
24  EC:    y^2 = x^3 + 19172747724480714596642200992274915039784641054455728765
25         965062830314980820158078796591218274137288 43*x + 4982364160176115561
26         97079679917127823411572951385000931922417615982076447840635286930619
27         6262671626890
28  Order: 9091997915950272182919811741783277234032768689196371505570607873311 2
29         5923009305159387323025071752049 0
30  ===== 3 =====
31  q:     11364997394937840228649764677229096542540960861494720411810283282904
32         5818883152209468652207180315659 3
33  P:     (56466397296285728483229561701550212037229798716830096107720437741 76
34          34204062934581680105576815725394,4590981462210374130006474344558760
35          1639042244938604606770009396809750335909385122149492970532993402 6,1)
36  EC:    y^2 = x^3 + 11570751228340212406581830107342138608501615935834402338
37         99707814734290579308905084972702437868132 03*x + 53791928627479281155
38         99881837238693838323804889824279393807264357121448087082310871711664
39         27388957817
40  Order: 9091997915950272182919811741783277234032768689195776329448226626323 6
41         6550652176757492176574425252744
42  ===== 4 =====
43  ...
44  ===== 32 =====
45  q:     792241
46  P:     (33183959,107785,1)
47  EC:    y^2 = x^3 + 27354579*x + 18197763
48  Order: 36443086
49  ===== 33 =====
50  q:     2477
51  P:     (165485,615671,1)
52  EC:    y^2 = x^3 + 590692*x + 134366
53  Order: 792640
54  ===== 34 =====
55  q:     127
56  P:     (1176,674,1)
57  EC:    y^2 = x^3 + 1026*x + 1793
58  Order: 2540
```

Listing 4.11: Certificate of Atkin-Morain test for a larger number

That is, since 127 is a prime number, then 8182798124355244964627830567604949510629
49182027658807300275915157441548137465525182317273409136750003 is a prime number.

A challenge in the ECPP algorithms, especially in Atkin-Morain's case is to identify a prime divisor q. We are using Pollard $p-1$ algorithm. Since Goldwasser-Kilan's algorithm is bounded by the point counting algorithm[45], we use small numbers and this works fine. Actually for Atkin-Morain's algorithm the next step would be to improve the identification process for the prime divisor q. We will not do this here, since the purpose of this chapter was mainly to give a structural idea of how CM-curves may be used in an practical problem like primality proving. In spite of it all, the implemented Atkin-Morain's algorithm for this thesis works very well for numbers up to 130 digits.

In the next section, we will analyze the run-time behavior of Atkin-Morain's ECPP with respect to Weierstraß curve and twisted Edwards curve.

4.4. Run-time behavior of Atkin-Morain's ECPP with respect to Weierstraß curve vs. twisted Edwards curve

Atkin-Morain's ECPP uses CM-curves for primality proving and these curves are in Weierstraß form. Twisted Edwards curves have some arithmetical advantages[46] compared to Weierstraß curves. Therefore, before processing the point multiplication (Proposition 4.2.1), we try to transform the Weierstraß curve to a twisted Edwards curve and do the point multiplication with the twisted Edwards curve. If we can not find a twisted Edwards curve, we carry on as usual with the Weierstraß curve. With this configuration we expect a speed advantage for Atkin-Morain's ECPP algorithm.

In this section, we will check this assumption by measuring and comparing the run-time behavior of Atkin-Morain's ECPP for both curve configurations.

For an empirical run-time measurement of Atkin-Morain's ECPP with respect to Weierstraß curve vs. twisted Edwards curve, we use a *2.4-GHz CORE i5 notebook with 64-Bit architecture and 8GB memory.*

4.4.1. Run-time measuring configuration

We process two run-time measurements. First with standard configuration, i.e Weierstraß curves and then with twisted Edwards curves. For each measurement, we generate 10 probable prime numbers from 16 bit size up to 336 bit size in 16 bit size steps. Throughout, there are 210 probable prime numbers to prove for each configuration.

There are three measuring points during one down-run step. The first one is the time consumed by curve construction, denoted by t_{EC}. The second one is the time consumed by the transformation from Weierstraß curve to twisted Edwards curve, denoted by t_T. And the third

---

[45]Notice, Schoof's algorithm is not implemented.
[46]See [5].

measuring points is the time consumed by point multiplication, denoted t_P. The run-time is measured in milliseconds. Note, $t_T = 0ms$ for Weierstraß configuration.

The time used for running one complete Atkin-Morain's ECPP algorithm is given by the following formula:

$$t_{ECPP} = \sum_{i=1}^{\#(\text{down-run steps})} (t_{EC_i} + t_{T_i} + t_{P_i}). \tag{4.5}$$

For example, we proof with Atkin Morain's ECPP a probable prime 9401456134553804117 for twisted Edwards configuration and get the certificate in Listing 4.12. Note, for run-time measurements we extended the certificate by twisted Edwards curve, t_{EC}, t_T and t_P.

```
Bit: 64 n: 9401456134553804117
===== 1 =====
q:      5442102803
P:      (7973293004720551298,5107724608470499134,1)
EC:     y^2 = x^3 + 3574727876049051131*x + 3858194832795572767
Order: 9401456131997236028
TE: (2340534170747735793*x^2 + y^2) = 1 + 5700014173324735663*x^2*y^2
tEC: 81
tT: 20
TP: 2
===== 2 =====
q:      9431593
P:      (5260027344,575252360,1)
EC:     y^2 = x^3 + 3176058941*x + 1510695908
Order: 5442029161
TE: null
tEC: 10
tT: 5
TP: 1
===== 3 =====
q:      117899
P:      (3291188,2554404,1)
EC:     y^2 = x^3 + 6026145*x + 15606
Order: 9431920
TE: (5958234*x^2 + y^2) = 1 + 2316534*x^2*y^2
tEC: 5
tT: 7
TP: 0
===== 4 =====
q:      4561
P:      (40721,81336,1)
EC:     y^2 = x^3 + 109311*x + 45025
Order: 118586
TE: null
tEC: 7
tT: 5
TP: 0
===== 5 =====
```

```
39  q:      233
40  P:      (1103,1545,1)
41  EC:     y^2 = x^3 + 709*x + 2568
42  Order: 4660
43  TE: (1239*x^2 + y^2) = 1 + 2345*x^2*y^2
44  tEC: 3
45  tT: 4
46  TP: 0
```

Listing 4.12: Atkin-Morain ECPP with twisted Edwards configuration for probable prime 9401456134553804117

For this example, we have

$$
\begin{aligned}
t_{EC} &= 81ms + 10ms + 5ms + 7ms + 3ms = 106ms \\
t_T &= 20ms + 5ms + 7ms + 5ms + 4ms = 41ms \\
t_P &= 2ms + 1ms + 5ms + 0ms + 0ms = 8ms
\end{aligned}
$$

The overall run-time is $t_{ECPP} = 155ms$.

Note, from the five down-run steps in this example, two Weierstraß curves have no twisted Edwards curve[47]. In spite of it all, we are consuming time for searching the twisted Edwards curve.

For each bit size in both configurations, we have 10 time measurements. We compute the average run-time for each bit size.

4.4.2. Run-time measuring results

By run-time measurement we confirm that the point multiplication with twisted Edwards curves is indeed faster than with Weierstraß curves. In Figure 4.1, we compare both curves with respect to point multiplication for twisted Edwards configuration.

With increasing bit size, twisted Edwards curve become more efficient. If the transformation to twisted Edwards curve is not successful, we carry on with Weierstraß curve. In such a case, the time to do the transformation is wasted.

From 3009 Weierstraß curves, 1116 curves were transformable to twisted Edwards curves, this is about 37% success. Approximately in 63% of the cases we waste time with respect to transformation.

For twisted Edwards configuration, we add the time for transformation and point multiplication $(t_T + t_P)$ and compare the result with point multiplication for Weierstraß configuration (Figure 4.2).

101

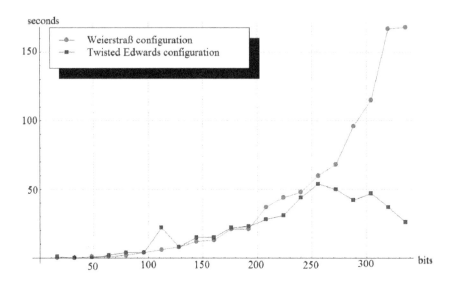

Figure 4.1.: Point multiplication Weierstraß vs. twisted Edwards

The advantage of faster point multiplication for twisted Edwards curve is lost, since the transformation is indeed time consuming.

In Figure 4.3, we compare for Weierstraß configuration the run-time of curve construction with CM-method and point multiplication.

In Figure 4.4, we compare for twisted Edwards configuration the run-time of curve construction with CM-method and transformation plus point multiplication.

In both configurations the time consumed for curve construction is considerably larger then the time consumed for point multiplication and transformation.

Finally, we compare in Figure 4.5 the overall time (t_{ECPP}) for both configurations.

We conclude: using twisted Edwards curves for Atkin-Morain's ECPP did not show any significant speed advantage with respect to Weierstraß curves.

---

[47] See Section 2.6.3.3.

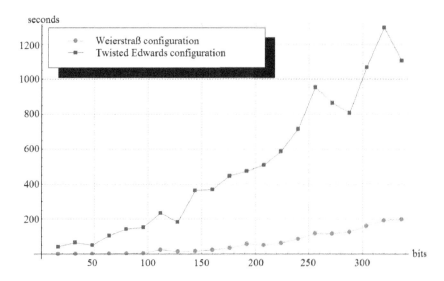

Figure 4.2.: Point multiplication Weierstraß vs. transformation and point multiplication twisted Edwards

4.5. Conclusion to chapter elliptic curve primality proving

In this chapter we introduced and implemented the ECPP algorithms due to Goldwasser-Kilian and Atkin-Morain. The difference between this two ECPP algorithms is the curve construction method.

Goldwasser-Kilian's ECPP counts the points on a randomly constructed elliptic curve over $\mathbb{F}_q$. To show the concept of Goldwasser-Kilian's ECPP, we rudimentary implemented a point counting algorithm based on Legendre symbol. Far more efficient implementation of Goldwasser-Kilian's ECPP could be realized by deploying Schoof's algorithm.

Atkin-Morains's ECPP is a primality proving algorithm that applies CM-method for curve construction. We completely implemented this algorithm in this thesis and we are able to prove probable prime numbers up to 130 digits.

Finally, we analyzed the run-time behaviour of Atkin-Morains's ECPP by transforming the Weierstraß curve into twisted Edwards curve in the CM-method. The point multiplication on a twisted Edwards curve is indeed faster than on a Weierstraß curve. But the transformation process from Weierstraß curve to twisted Edwards curve eliminates this advantage. In particular, the time consumed by curve construction with CM-method is several times larger than the point multiplication on the constructed curve. Therefore, deploying twisted Edwards curves

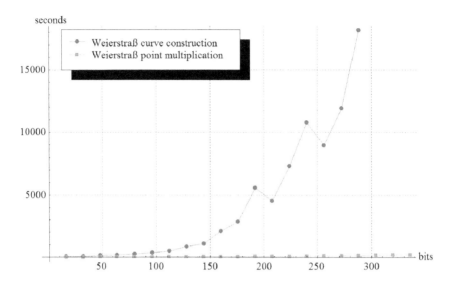

Figure 4.3.: Relation for Weierstraß configuration

in Atkin-Morain's ECPP algorithm did not increase the efficiency of the run-time. At least, not in the interval for prime numbers from 16 bit up to 336 bit.

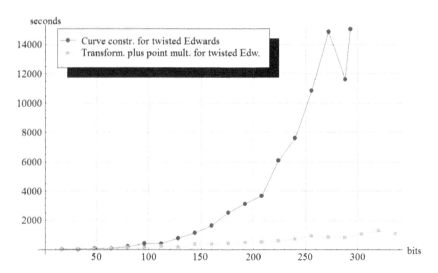

Figure 4.4.: Relation for twisted Edwards configuration

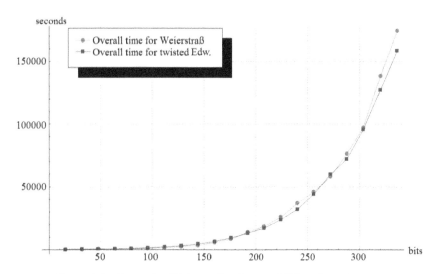

Figure 4.5.: Comparing Weierstraß and twisted Edwards configuration

Chapter 5.

Conclusion

Based on the theory of elliptic curves, we designed an object-oriented model that reflects the arithmetical properties of elliptic curves. This elliptic curve model is designed as a general Java interface. Methods in this interface are for example `add`, `subtract`, `multiply`, `jInvariant`, `randomCurve`, `randomPoint`, `toAffineCoordinates`, etc.

While the interface has a general structure, the first base implementation restricts the field to be finite. Every additional implementation is an extension from this base implementation and inherits the finite field property.

We created an elliptic curve for the short Weierstraß form and for the twisted Edwards form as an extension of this base implementation. In addition, we developed a utility program to transform a twisted Edwards curve to a Weierstraß curve and vice versa, although, the transformation from Weierstraß curve to twisted Edwards curve is not always possible. In fact, we observed that only 37% of Weierstraß curves are transformable.

We called this model an *elliptic curve arithmetic system*. This is basically an implementation of the composition law which is the group operation on the elliptic curve.

The *elliptic curve arithmetic system* is extensible by design. For example, if we want to implement another elliptic curve form, like the Montgomery form, then we have to inherit from the base implementation.

Built on the *elliptic curve arithmetic system*, we developed three curve construction methods. The curve construction method consists of finding an elliptic curve over a finite field together with the order. The constructed curve will be naturally given in Weierstraß form.

In the first curve construction method, the field order is given as an input value. The curve itself is generated randomly. To identify the order, we rely on point counting. For that we implemented the Legendre symbol, which is not efficient since we have to check all the quadratic residues. This leads to an upper limit of constructable curves with approximately $5 \cdot 10^6$ points. An improvement of point counting could be achieved with Schoof's algorithm. However, the main focus of this thesis is to construct elliptic curves with the CM-method, which is implemented in the second construction method.

In the CM-method the field order is also given as an input value. For a given field order, we find a valid fundamental discriminant to determine the value of trace of Frobenius. The trace of Frobenius and the field order delivers the order of the curve. We solve the remaining of finding the parameters of the curve by using Hilbert class polynomials. With the implemented version of the CM-method, we are able to construct curves with curve orders up to 10^{900} points.

As a proof of concept, we implemented a third curve construction method. In contrast to the other two methods the input is the order of the curve. By choosing random values for the order of the field in a narrow interval, we generate random eliptic curves and check if the given curve order fits to the randomly generated elliptic curve. This method has an upper limit of constructable curves with approximately $5 \cdot 10^8$ points.

As an application of the curve construction methods we developed two primality proving algorithms based on ECPP. The first one, Goldwasser-Kilian's ECPP algorithm applies the first construction method and can be considered as a introduction to Atkin-Morain's ECPP. Atkin-Morain's ECPP algorithm is identical to Goldwasser-Kilian's ECPP, but uses the CM-method for curve construction. With Atkin-Morain's ECPP we were able to prove the primality of a given number up to 130 digits.

We used the flexibility of the object-oriented programming to decide whether the use of twisted Edwards form can accelerate the Atkin-Morain's ECPP algorithm. With minimal programming efforts, we were able to determin that the advantage of twisted Edwards point multiplication, at least for numbers less than 150 digits, is negligible with respect to the main response of the algorithm. Apart from that, the gain of twisted Edwards point multiplication is more then outweighed by the search for possible transformability of the curve.

107

Appendix A.

List of notation

$E(K)$	Set of all K-rational points (x,y) on the elliptic curve
E/K	Elliptic curve E defined over an arbitrary field K
O	Identity element on $E(K)$
$\mathbb{P}_K^2$	Projective plane over K
$char(K)$	Characteristic of field K
Δ	Discriminant of the elliptic curve
S^1	Circle group
G_2	Group of order 2
Λ	Fundamental parallelogram
L	Lattice
$\wp$	Weierstraß $\wp$-function
$E(\mathbb{Q}_{tors})$	Torsion subgroup of $E(\mathbb{Q})$
$\mathbb{F}_q$	Finite field with $q = p^k$ and p prime
$\#E(\mathbb{F}_q)$	Order or cardinality of an elliptic curve E over $\mathbb{F}_q$
$End(E(K))$	Endomorphism ring of E over K
ϕ_q	Frobenius map
$f(X)$	Polynomial
$K[X]$	Ring of polynomial defined over K
deg	Degree
ker	Kernel
$\bar{K}$	Algebraic closure of K
$a \mid b$	a divides b
$\left(\frac{n}{q}\right)$	Legendre symbol
t	Trace of Frobenius
D	Fundamental discriminant
F	Imaginary quadratic field
$\mathcal{O}_F$	Maximal order of an imaginary quadratic field F

Appendix A. List of notation

$\mathfrak{a}, \mathfrak{b}, \dots$	Ideals
$\mathcal{C}(\mathcal{O}_F)$	Ideal class group
$h(\mathcal{O}_F), h(D)$	Class number
(a, b, c)	Binary quadratic short form
$H_D(x)$	Hilbert class polynomial
$j(\tau)$	j-function
CM	Complex multiplication
ECPP	Elliptic curve primality proving

Appendix B.

Software infrastructure

All algorithms in this thesis are implemented with Java 1.6.0_23. For development environment we used Eclipse Platform (Version: 3.7.0, Build id: I20110613-1736)[48].

The following external frameworks/libraries are part of the software.

1. spring Release 3.0.5 (http://www.springsource.org/node/2880)

2. xstream 1.2.2 (http://xstream.codehaus.org/)

3. apfloat 1.5.2 (http://www.apfloat.org/)

4. junit 4.7 (http://www.junit.org/node/574)

5. commons-logging 1.1.1 (http://commons.apache.org/logging/)

6. log4j 1.2.13 (http://logging.apache.org/log4j/)

The build tool is Apache Maven 2.2.1 (http://maven.apache.org/).

The software development methodology is based on *test driven development* and the main design pattern which is used is the *inversion of control* pattern.

---

[48]http://www.eclipse.org/

Bibliography

[1] A.O.L.Atkin, F.Morain, Elliptic curves and Primality Proving, Math. Comp. , 61, 29-67, 1993

[2] J.V.Belding, Curves, Cryptography, and Prime of the Form $x^2 + y^2 D$. University of Maryland, Department of Mathematics, 2008.

[3] J.V.Belding, R.Bröker, A.Enge, and K.Lauter, Computing Hilbert class of polynomials, Algorithmic Number Theory Symposium-ANTS VIII (A. J. van der Poorten and A. Stein, eds.), Lecture Notes in Computer Science, vol. 5011, Springer, 2008, pp. 282-295.

[4] D.J.Bernstein, T.Lange, and C.Peters. Faster addition and doubling on elliptic curves. In ASIACRYPT 2007, volume 4833 of LNCS, pages 29-50. Springer, 2007.

[5] D.J.Bernstein, P.Birkner, M.Joye, T.Lange, and C.Peters. Twisted Edwards curves. In AFRICACRYPT 2008, volume 5023 of LNCS, pages 389-405. Springer, 2008.

[6] I.Blake, G.Seroussi, N.Smart, Elliptic Curves in Cryptography, London Mathematical Society, Lecture Note Series 265, Cambridge University Press 2002.

[7] S.Bosch, Algebra, Springer-Verlag Berlin Heidelberg, Sechste Auflage 2006.

[8] R.Bröker, Constructing elliptic curves of prescribed order, PhD Thesis, Thomas Stieltjes Institute for Mathematics, 2006.

[9] R.Bröker, Constructing supersingular elliptic curves, Journal of Combinatorics and Number Theory 1, Volume 1, Issue 3, pp. 269-273, 2009.

[10] H.Cohen, A Course in Computational Algebraic Number Theory, Springer Graduate Texts in Mathematics, 3rd Corr. ed., 1993.

[11] K.Conrad, Separability, Expository papers, http://www.math.uconn.edu/~kconrad/blurbs/, viewed on 10/12/2011.

[12] D.Cox, Primes of the Form $x^2 + ny^2$: Fermat, Class Field Theory and Complex Multiplication, John Wiley & Sons, 1989.

[13] R.Crandall, C.B.Pomerance, Prime Numbers: A Computational Perspective, Springer New York, 2nd ed., 2005.

[14] R.Dedekind, R.G.L.Dirichlet, Vorlesungen über Zahlentheorie, Braunschweig, Vieweg und Sohn. Dritte umgearbeitete und vermehrte Auflage, 1879.

[15] H.M.Edwards (4/9/2007), A normal form for elliptic curves, Bulletin of the American Mathematical Society (Providence, R.I.: American Mathematical Society) 44: 393-422.

[16] E.Freitag, R.Busam, Funktionentheorie 1, Springer-Verlag Berlin Heidelberg, 4th ed., 2006. Chapman & Hall / CRC, 2008.

[17] S.Goldwasser, J.Kilian Primality Testing based on Elliptic Curves. Journal of the ACM, vol. 46, no. 4, pages 450-472, July 1999.

[18] S.Kim, Special values of j-function which are algebraic. http://www.math.ucla.edu/~i707107/205b2.pdf, viewed on 28/12/2011.

[19] A.W.Knapp, Elliptic Curves, Princeton University Press, Mathematical Notes 40, 1992.

[20] F.Morain, Implementation of the Atkin-Goldwasser-Kilian Primality Testing Algorithm, Rapport de Recherche 911, INRIA, Oct. 1989.

[21] K.Okeya, H.Kurumatani, K.Sakurai. Elliptic Curves with Montgomery-Form and Their Cryptographic Applications. PKC 2000, LNCS 1751, pp. 238-257, 2000.

[22] R.Scherz, Complex Multiplication, New Mathematical Monographs: 15, Cambridge University Press, 2008.

[23] A.Schmidt, Einführung in die algebraische Zahlentheorie, Springer Lehrbuch, Springer-Verlag Berlin Heidelberg, 2007.

[24] R.Schoof, Counting Points on Elliptic Curves over Finite Fields. J. Theor. Nombres Bordeaux 7, pages 219-254, 1995.

[25] J.P.Serre, et al., Seminar on Complex Multiplication, Lecture Notes in Mathematics, Princeton, N.J. 1957-58, Springer Verlag, 1966.

[26] J.H.Silverman, J.Tate, Rational Points on Elliptic Curves, Springer Undergraduate Texts in Mathematics, 1992.

[27] J.H.Silverman, The Arithmetic of Elliptic Curves, Springer Graduate Texts in Mathematics, Vol. 106, 1986.

[28] J.H.Silverman, Advances Topics in the Arithmetic of Elliptic Curves, Springer Graduate Texts in Mathematics, Vol. 151, 1999.

[29] A.V.Sutherland, Computing Hilbert class polynomials with the Chinese Remainder Theorem, Mathematics of Computation 80 (2011), pp. 501-538.

[30] L.C.Washington, Elliptic Curves - Number Theory and Cryptography, Discrete Mathematics and its Applications, Chapman & Hall / CRC, 2008.

www.ingramcontent.com/pod-product-compliance
Lightning Source LLC
LaVergne TN
LVHW042338060326

832902LV00006B/242